Disturbers of the Peace

Disturbers of the Peace
Profiles in Nonadjustment

Colman McCarthy

With a Foreword by Robert Coles

A Washington Post Book

HOUGHTON MIFFLIN COMPANY
BOSTON 1973

First Printing c

ISBN: 0-395-15466-9
Library of Congress Catalog Card Number: 72-9014
Printed in the United States of America

For Mavourneen, whose husband I am

Not to be mad would be another form of madness.
— Pascal

Acknowledgments

I AM GRATEFUL to Philip Geyelin, editor of the editorial page of the Washington *Post*. Many know him as a man of intelligence and grace but I know him also — through contact in the daily rush of helping put out a newspaper — as a man of compassion. Much of the material gathered for this book first appeared, in different form, on the *Post*'s editorial page, and did so by his kindness and encouragement. Phil Geyelin is the rare editor who gives his writers not only time to dig and compose, but also time to think.

Others to whom I am indebted, both for help in writing this book and for past generosity in helping me understand the vocation of a writer, include Howard Simons and Morton Mintz of the Washington *Post,* Gilbert Harrison of the *New Republic,* Sargent Shriver, the Trappist community in Conyers, Georgia, Alice and Tom Deegan of Greenwich, Connecticut, Gene Patterson of the St. Petersburg *Times,* Jack Griffin of United Press International, Bernard Shulman, Mary Picone and Beatrice Thomas of Glen Head, New York, and Anne Barrett of Houghton Mifflin.

My mother and three brothers, in the best traditions of Irish families and the treatment of last sons, have been my most constant but most appreciated critics. My deepest debt is to my wife, Mavourneen. She wisely stayed clear of all rough drafts, made no suggestions on content, and had little concern that the book ever be finished; her passion instead was seeing that the main goals of our life were kept in steady progress — raising our children, sharing our days and nights, staying on the ground. She believed I'd finish this work sooner and more tidily if I did it myself, a notion she also has about her own work when I offer to help do the bills, the marketing, or clean up the Monday dirties. I'll never know if I'd have written a better book had she been "the good little helpmate" American wives are conditioned to be, sadly so, but I know that her work — as important as anything destined for a library shelf — could not be improved on. Nor could anything else about her.

Foreword by Robert Coles

IN THE EARLY 1960s I was trying to learn how black and white children in rural and urban Georgia, North Carolina, and Louisiana managed the stresses of desegregation, and I was also trying to get some sense of how their families lived — and were challenged by the social and political changes initiated so often by young activists, whom I was also observing, but also working with. By "activists" I mean the men and women who made up CORE or SNCC, who had left classrooms in order to assert their rights as American citizens — and for doing so, of course, they were called anything and everything by people in charge of defending the status quo, among whom I came to realize a good number of my psychiatric colleagues. I went along, too: for more months than I now care to remember I summoned all of those labels I had acquired in hospitals and clinics — until reporters and editors from the Atlanta *Constitution* and the Nashville *Tennessean* (whatever it lacks, the South has many fine newspapers) began to make me stop and think a little. I have in mind a long conversation I had in 1962 with Ralph McGill. I was in his Atlanta office and he was being courteous and deferential to me. Would I like something more to drink? Had I been to X or Y and what did I think of those cities? Won't you please hurry up with your work, because we all need to know so much about the South's people, especially its children and youth? And, by the way, what do you think about some of the young people who are doing those sit-ins and journeying on those freedom rides?

I had my thoughts; I spoke with a certain clinical sharp-
ness, or so I imagined, and I no doubt showed Mr. McGill, a
mere newspaperman, a daily columnist, how much I had discovered, how little escaped my medical and psychiatric eye.
Politely he nodded, again thanked me for being there (in the
South as well as in his office) and in a most quiet and humble
voice begged to offer this observation: "I'm only a newspaperman, of course, but I've spent some time poking around, talking with various individuals, like you do, and a lot of the
civil rights people I've met are brave enough to make me
feel ashamed of myself. Maybe, as you say, some of them do
have their problems. But what about the rest of us — who
don't question things and fight the injustice which is everywhere? What kind of problems do *we* have?"

As I read Colman McCarthy's book I found myself wishing
that Ralph McGill were alive to get acquainted with this
gifted and sensitive writer, this tough and searching social
observer. Mr. McGill's columns, day in and day out located
on the left side of the Atlanta *Constitution*'s front page, were
an enormous force for enlightenment in Georgia; and Mr.
McCarthy's writing in the Washington *Post* as well as in some
of our national magazines is very much in that tradition:
clarifying, both morally instructive and factually sound — in
sum, an educational experience for the reader. One finishes
his book a little more aware, a little less protected by the
temptation to inertia and smugness I fear most of us yield to
rather often. A black mother in rural Georgia — only fifty
miles from the monastery the author of this book tells us he
came to know for five years — once said this to me about Mr.
McGill's articles, and I believe she would want me to use her
words here, as a means of doing justice to Mr. McCarthy: "I
read him and I pinch myself and I say he's over there in
Atlanta doing his writing, and he's such a decent man, such
an intelligent man, and there are lots like me (little people,

people most of those politicians, so very big and important, don't care anything about, except to hoodwink us into voting for them once, twice, thrice), and all of us can read him and say yes, you're right, and yes, keep going, yes, Mr. teacher, yes, Mr. honest-to-God, good human being, keep going, because you lift my spirits up and help my mind stay awake. You write and the next thing I know, I'm thinking about what you wrote in between doing my living for the day."

The essays in this book need no comment from me; each one of them stands by itself, a luminous and moving effort to show how particular individuals from several parts of this country have challenged all sorts of "powers and principalities," thereby becoming Mr. McCarthy's "disturbers of the peace." But I do think I ought to respond to the essential message that binds these essays, pointedly summarized in the quote from Pascal at the beginning of the book — and how refreshing to find a journalist of broad religious sensibility drawing upon Pascal instead of R. D. Laing for the message that the "well-adjusted" and thoroughly "sane" can in their own way be madly indifferent, barbarously uninterested in their neighbor's plight, not to mention stupidly (perhaps it can be said insanely) unaware of their own. In a sense these portraits of stubbornly idiosyncratic, proud men and women are "case studies," descriptions of people "crazy" enough not to let go, not to stop saying what they believe, not to stop shaking their fists at company bureaucrats and government officials and elected representatives, and beyond all of "them," at us, the general public, as we are so often called — ordinary men and women who too easily shrug our shoulders and go along with what seems to be the inevitable if not the desirable. In this regard people like me are very helpful; we provide a veneer of scientific sanction, however flimsy and inappropriate, for those who simply don't want their "adjustment" to what psychiatrists call "reality" (what a multitude of sins can be tucked into that word!) in any way threatened.

So it was in the early 1960s that civil rights activists of both races were described (by people more "refined" or educated than those outspoken, segregationist "rednecks") as "antisocial" or "delinquent" or "psychopathic" or "violence-prone" — and needless to say, "emotionally disturbed." A number of youths I knew rather well were sent away for "observation" at state hospitals; several times I sat in a county court and heard for myself those determined, unrelenting young men and women called not troublemakers, but "candidates for psychiatric evaluation." Nor can I say I was as quick as Mr. McCarthy to sense the irony, if not outright scandal, I was witness to; more often than I care to admit I found myself wondering whether there just might be some truth to those allegations. Naturally, I was against the prosecutors and the obviously biased judges, often enough admitted, unashamed members of white Citizens Councils; and yet, I couldn't stop myself every once in a while from looking askance at those whose ideals I wholeheartedly supported. Why *were* they doing all of this — taking on the police and the courts, risking their educational careers, incurring not only the wrath of the white world, but the suspicion and even resentment (all too often, alas) of black people who had long ago given up any real hope that they, like other Americans, might one day be full-fledged citizens?

Even as I read this book I found myself (for a moment, and in the back of my mind) wondering about the extraordinary psychiatrist the author brings to us — a doctor who worked exceptionally long and hard with an apparently hopeless child, so badly damaged at such an early age. I do not want to be disingenuous; I admire that doctor, even as the author does. But I rather suspect most of us, maybe all of us, find ourselves to some extent, even if briefly, fearing if not resenting men and women like him — or Dorothy Day, or

Thomas Merton, or the less renowned but no less honorable and idealistic people who appear in the pages to follow. They are all brought to life and given a voice by a writer whom one, finally, judges to be one of the people he describes, a writer who disturbs our peace, makes our complacency feel indecent, our acquiescence a scandal, our submission a tragedy for us, never mind those "others" whose suffering we try so hard to ignore or rationalize away as inevitable, as simply "part of life."

They are, in a way, literally frightening people — the bus driver, the ice-cream maker, the monk, the doctor, the man who lost his son and never quite went through one of those successful "grief reactions" we are all urged to have when tragedy strikes. We are made afraid by a standard of conduct we know to be rare. What might we do were we braver? And in between the lines we meet an observer who has chosen to pay those he spends time with such loving attention; he stands respectfully beside them, and he, too, demonstrates in his own quiet, understated way what each of us, of whatever profession or occupation, might also do if we wished — at the very least, heed these particular people, these various "disturbers of the peace," and in doing so affirm our own dignity. Many of us will have no trouble seeing a certain redemptive grace in some of the lives Colman McCarthy offers us here. Perhaps those written about were more than simply thankful for the unexpected and occasionally decisive help a journalist saw fit to extend. Perhaps they, too, saw a touch of redemptive grace before them, not on the pages of a book, but earlier on, in the presence of a man who has a very special sense of what a "newspaper story" is all about.

Contents

Introduction

DRAMATIC STORIES are near endless of hunters caught in mountain blizzards, or weekend sailors losing their way in strange sea tides, or travelers running out of fuel between oases in a desert, and how, bucking the odds of death, the heroes end up beating them and living. Marked by circumstances for tragedy, they adjusted to impossible conditions — no water supply in one case, no food in another, no hope in all of them. But they fought to live, and did. It is an old story, man's ability to adjust, his instinct for living with great torture until relief comes. Human beings can often rest their heads on the most brutal stones of suffering and adjust well to the hard pillow.

Journalists who come upon these stories are lucky; they not only get a jump on the accepted beat but they also have a chance to get out from under the always falling guillotine of deadlines to wonder at deep instincts and rare graces. Most of us in the newsrooms, though, never come on men and women who adjust heroically to terror. Years ago, this would have been a loss, one more yawn to endure in a sometimes sleepy business. But lately, or at least in the kind of stories many journalists are now assigned to, or stumble upon themselves, another kind of hero is appearing: the man or woman who refuses to adjust. These differ from the classic heroes because the powers defied are not those of a wrathful snowstorm or shifty sea but the more dangerous forces that the rest of us, fearing rough body contact with society, learn little by little to live with. This includes everything from great horrors like corporate irresponsibility, militarism, pollution of the land, and government deception, to the small daily irks and gyps, such as ice cream containing 50 per cent air, expensive shoes that come unsewn after a month, contaminated meat, week-old cars already needing repairs of repairs. We have adjusted so easily to these great and small adversities that, with no trumpets or headlines heralding the terror, the abnormal has become the normal. The worst horror is not that tragedies are inflicted upon us but that, with no fight and sometimes no murmur, we learn calmly to live with them. We cut our values into usable lengths and throw the rest into a pile, leaving our integrity clothed only in bare shreds. If asked, we say, well, it's the new look.

Because adjustment is made in small fits, we see each giving-in as only a small cave-in, not a big one. If pollution, to take one horror that threatens us, came in killer doses, then we would fight back. But why sweat the small losses? Adjustment is easier. For example, a city park is taken over for a new highway that the concrete lobby decides is needed, so the neighborhood people adjust and use another park a mile away. A stream through that park has been contaminated by the town's power plant, so the people are told to fish upstream, 30 miles away. They go upstream, but a chemical factory blackens the air there with smoke, so breathing is bad. They are told to go across the state line 100 miles away, where tougher clean-air laws exist. They go, but a new airport for jumbo jets is going up. The noise prevents sleeping at night. In desperation, but still adjusting, they decide to go 2000 miles away, to buy some land in the remote hills of the north country. When they arrive, the air, earth, and water are clean all right, but the spread of land they bought has a new neighbor: the Defense Department, which, in a mad foam, is building ABM silos. Each movement in this march to tragedy was made in Japanese-size steps, short and quick, that add up when no one is looking.

The statistics of pollution — to stay on this for a moment — show that we've been adjusting well. Much of America lives comfortably with the following:

1. Of the nation's drinking water, 50 per cent has been discharged only a few hours earlier from some industrial or municipal sewer. In the last ten years, 128 known outbreaks of diseases or poisoning have been caused by contaminated drinking water.

2. Pesticides killed six million fish in one recent year.

3. Strip mining may soon claim 71,000 square miles of American land, an area the size of Pennsylvania and West Virginia combined.

4. In one Washington, D.C., inner-city neighborhood, 25 per cent of the children tested under six showed high levels of lead in the blood. The source is now seen to be not only paint, which the children eat, but inhaled air made foul by car exhaust containing lead.

5. By 1976, we will have the disposal problem of 58 billion nonreturnable bottles and cans.

6. Forty million pounds of dog dung are deposited annually on New York City streets.

That most people become good sheep or good Germans and adjust to these horrors may be a tribute to human flexibility. But isn't something subtracted from the sum of the person's individuality and emotions? A clear equation is created: adjust to the subhuman and you may become subhuman too. No one is going to regress to become King Kong overnight, but the chance for some loss in humanity is present. For a common example, cities are so clogged with cars that the pressure of the morning and evening traffic jam easily goads many usually mild people into savage aggression. This citizen is common. He blares the horn feverishly if you happen to doze when the light turns green, he wildly cuts you off to get into your lane because it looks faster — but never is — he gives you the finger on passing back into his

lane, he shouts a curse at you at the light. These still-life
scenes are part of the daily urbanscape, brushstrokes of hatred. Yet an hour later, who is home playing gently with his
kids, talking sweetly with his wife, his face calm and happy
with no twitching of traffic-jam anger? It's King Kong, but
now he's changed into a lamb again. He was an animal for
thirty minutes, but what is that?

Adjustment comes in many forms. Much of it results from
laziness — better to yield than fight — but much also is
caused by other reasons. The inner-city poor, who must suffer pollution, marketplace fraud, political corruption, and
other evils at their most fetid, often have no choice except
adjustment to their conditions. Jerome Kretchmer, head of
New York City's Environmental Protection Administration,
tells about a ghetto mother who was seen "air mailing" her
garbage. She puts her refuse into bags and hurls them from
her tenement window into the vacant lot below. When asked
why she air mailed, Kretchmer told the Senate Subcommittee
on the Environment that she "said she used to carry her garbage down the four flights but she grew afraid of running
the gauntlet of addicts roaming the hallways of her building,
and afraid of a rat attacking her child while she was doing
so. In other words, as offensive as air mailing is, it had a
sound internal logic according to the conditions under which
she was forced to live."

Another form of adjustment is the kind found not among
those trapped in the slums but among those comfortable in
the suburbs. During the political campaign of 1972, a few
grim words kept appearing and reappearing in the news reports from the cities and towns: skepticism, estrangement,
disenchantment, alienation, stagnation, disillusion. Reporters interviewing the voters talked about an epidemic of emotional deadness threatening the country; large numbers of voters were unable to be aroused, neither to disgust by the

charges of conniving and corruption among some officials in power nor aroused to hope by calls to reform from those out of power. The remarkable fact was not that many people were desensitized to tragedies like the war or unemployment; these were seen as abstractions far from the beats of daily life, issues to be debated, not horrors personally endured. The remarkable disturbance in our culture, then and now, is the desensitivity to what truly does touch us in our daily lives. It is hard, for example, to find anyone who cares even about the food he eats. The nation's annual dental bill is $4.5 billion; annual soft-drinks sales are $6 billion. Is it wild to put the two together and conclude that we are a nation of rotting teeth partly because we subject those teeth to vast amounts of useless sugar water — some 88 quarts a year per person? Even without "wild" thinking, we know that 57,000 deaths a year are directly caused by lung cancer from cigarettes. The packages warn us of the danger, yet 1972 saw an increase in the number of smokers.

If there is little personal concern among so many citizens about saving their own teeth and lungs, how can a population be aroused to saving its national soul? Most of us have become passive bystanders not only to the large deteriorations — a secretive government, our dropping a ton of bombs a minute on Vietnam, unemployment — we also passively witness deteriorations in our own personal lives, the one place presumably where people are not caged in powerlessness. To fight back, to resist the con games and shams, is almost to admit that you deliberately seek a life of frustration. You are fearless in the most reckless sense: you have no fear of failure when everything appears rigged to make failure certain. Skepticism, alienation, disillusion — what are these but handy reflex mechanisms to defend ourselves from the crushed feelings of possible defeat? The skeptic — by definition, a person who says, "I doubt that my caring or acting can make a difference" — can manage his feelings and interests, whereas the person who still cares or acts with hope risks repudiation.

Political campaigns do not uncover the sickness of passivity, they reveal the symptom only in one more way, highly visible: that many prefer adjustment to the abnormal rather than resistance. "What is new about our alienation," writes Kenneth Kenniston, a thoughtful psychiatrist, in his book *The Uncommitted,* "is not that the 'bottom' third of the population has little deep commitment to our society . . . but that a sense of estrangement pervades the rest of our society, an alienation that has few apparent roots in poverty, exclusion, sickness, oppression, lack of choice and opportunity." If Americans are not being crushed by the traditional weights of misery, it is not hard to look at people's lives and observe the new weights; they hang heavy. Many people are passive because little in their outer lives supplies the demands of their inner lives. Emptiness, boredom, and flatness naturally possess millions of citizens who earn their livings from empty, boring, and flat work. What can lifeless and inanimate computers, inventories, charts, records, typewriters, engines, reports, assembly lines, bureaus, appliances, or forms do to keep the spirit alive? Gone dry from so much lifelessness, no wonder people cannot respond with lively juices to call for reform. Any cupful of outrage a person might have must not be spilled at a political or corporate scandal; save it instead for rebelling against the office elevator that doesn't work or the evening traffic jam. Once at home, the person who survives his lifeless job and the creaky transportation to and from it, now unthinkingly eats lifeless factory food, and no doubt looks across the table at kids made inanimate by the stupor of television. Limpness and cheapness surround him, and how can all these loose contagious germs not spread the infection further.

In seeking cures for the epidemic, a childlike wishfulness often appears in many otherwise intelligent people: if only someone would rise among us who could free our country from this bondage. Naturally, the politicians play to this hunger, each claiming he is the shepherd who can find green pastures again. Be wary of mass solutions, warned Carl Jung, a source of clarity on the problem of adjustment. "All the highest achievements of virtue, as well as the blackest villainies, are individual. The larger a community is . . . the more will the individual be morally and spiritually crushed and, as a result, the one source of moral and spiritual progress for society is choked up . . . Any large company composed of wholly admirable persons has the morality and intelligence of an unwieldy, stupid and violent animal. The bigger the organization, the more unavoidable is its immorality and blind stupidity. Society, by automatically stressing all the collective qualities in its individuals, puts a premium on mediocrity, on everything that settles down to vegetate in an easy, irresponsible way. Individuality will inevitably be driven to the wall. This process begins in school, continues at the university, and rules in all departments in which the State has a hand. In a small social body, the individuality of its members is better safeguarded; and the greater is their relative freedom and the possibility of conscious responsibility."

Jung has something. Around the country, the citizens who have not yet caved in to estrangement, ones who refuse to be clamped dead in the teeth of adjustment, can usually be found operating alone or in some small grouping, where personal conscience still counts and risks are not feared. In the past few years, with the benefit of good luck and good editors — reporters need both or else their journalism becomes secretarial work — I have come upon a number of common and mostly unknown people who quietly took stances of noncompliance. They reached a point where they saw exactly the kind of hell they were being led into by some corporate, political, or social devil, and said no. They refused adjustment to some form of cheapness, guff, crime, grossness, or to some kind of debasement in values that struck them as brazenly wrong. These lions of nonadjustment who prowl a lonely path of protest or resistance did not have ferocious origins. Most of them came from the schools, shops, offices, farms, and homes where the rest of us live. One man, a school-bus driver, whose new General Motors buses kept breaking down, refused to adjust to the brush-offs of GM officials. A nearly illiterate mayor in a West Virginia mountain town refused to acclimate his lungs or his people to the polluted air from the local Union Carbide factory. An upholsterer in New Hampshire, whose child was tragically burned when his pajamas caught fire, refused to adjust to the horror that the textile industry, with the federal government's silent approval, continues to make clothing for other children that can be highly flammable. A Connecticut man, who lost a son by drowning when a negligent camp counselor took some campers down dangerous rapids, does not accept the lax safety standards that thousands of U.S. camps are allowed to get by with. A New York woman believes that children come before dogs. A Navy Department film maker quit the government because he could no longer stomach movies that glorified the Vietnam war. A neighborhood pastry maker insists that ice cream be of pure quality, even if he is the only one around who will make it that way. Another self-employed worker is a butcher who stood up to the meat-and-cattle industry and raises beef with no chemicals or additives. In Brooklyn, a psychiatrist would not accept the hopeless diagnosis on a child abused to near death by her parents. I would like to report that all those I have written about were successful in their nonadjustment, and thus make the point that nothing

can trip up the person of resolve. In truth, though, the
heavy news is different: some did not succeed. They got nowhere for their trouble. Some, like the West Virginia miner
whose resistance partly caused his death, were not only
tripped up but were harshly stepped on besides. The meek
may be scheduled to inherit the earth, but, not to despair in
any way, it doesn't look as if the inheritance will be soon.
Common to all those included here was the decision to stop
adjusting to the abnormal, a refusal to yield another inch so
that another mile could not be taken from them. That they
stand out at all may not be caused by the high polish of their
own beliefs but because of the dullness of everyone else's. As
Bernanos wrote in *Tradition of Freedom,* "the horrors which
we have seen, the still greater horrors which we shall presently see, are not signs that rebels, insubordinate, untameable
men, are increasing in constant numbers, but rather that
there is a constant increase, a stupendously rapid increase, in
the number of obedient, docile men."

With a repetition that almost became predictable, nearly
all of the nonadjusted men and women I have written about
observed about themselves, though in different phrasing,
"I must be crazy doing this." This self-questioning of sanity,
done jokingly, suggests the unfunny truth that their way of
life was a hard one, when the easier rounds of the adjusted
life could just as easily be made. A character in a T. S. Eliot
play believed that in a world of fugitives, the man running
in the opposite direction appears the madman. The question of who is sane in society is not always, if ever, a matter of
separating the population between those put away in institutions and those not. A mark of the supposedly stable person-
ality is calmness during a storm, an ability not to let the
world's cruelty in so close that it penetrates our defenses.
Yet it can be the other way. In *The Boston Strangler,* the
author tells how a psychiatrist named Leo Alexander ex-

amined some suspects. Dr. Alexander, Gerold Frank wrote, "often thought it ironic that if a depressed patient walked into his office and said the world was so grim that he could not face it, he had to treat him as a sick man. Actually, the patient was right. He saw the truth only too clearly. But he was labeled sick, because he had lost certain basic defenses . . . He no longer had the normal illusions that keep us sane."

The nonadjusting man or woman is not to be confused with the many mal-adjusteds. The latter reject all old values and cannot embrace any new ones; what works at the moment, or what feels good, is their standard. Contrasted, the nonadjusted person rejects only those values — and the powerful institutions pushing them — that cheapen life. The nonadjusted are often accused of bad will. James Roche, for example, when he was board chairman of General Motors, for which he still labors, regularly gave speeches defending the free-enterprise system, picking out for special whacks of denunciation some always nameless groups he believed were "the enemies of business." In fact, those whom Roche apparently had in mind may only have been enemies of businessmen who were proven enemies of the public — the businessmen who cheated, gulled, or injured the consumer. But taking advantage of the consumer — the latter is a part-time buyer up against full-time sellers — is now so common and normal that the consumers who will not adjust to this are seen as abnormal.

The difficulty of nonadjustment as a way of life has long concerned Rabbi Abraham Heschel, a hero to many who refuse to yield one kind of inch or another. He tells a story. Once upon a time in a kingdom long ago and far away, it happened that after the grain crop had been harvested and stored, it was discovered to be poison. Anyone who ate it went insane. The king and his advisers immediately took counsel as to what should be done. Clearly, not enough food was available from other sources to sustain the population. There was no choice but to eat the grain. Very well, the king decided, let us eat it. But at the same time we must feed a few people on a different diet so that there will be among us some who remember that we are insane.

The people I have written about are disturbers of the peace. Theirs is a vocation of paradox because in upsetting the adjustment patterns of the community an immense personal peace was gained. You gain peace by risking it. Most of us are glad if we can get meaning into our lives in only pill form, and only dream about larger doses. The people here believed passionately in what they were doing. Perhaps because of this I developed a fondness for all of them, and a trust also. Someone said to me that it's a conflict of interest for a journalist to become involved in the lives of those he writes about. Doubtlessly it is sometimes, but not here. There was not a conflict but a joining of interest. Why have a private vision unless you rejoice when you find others who share it.

COLMAN MCCARTHY

Washington, D.C.

PART I

Disturbing the Corporations

John Donovan

IN THE BOARD ROOMS of General Motors, the world's mightiest corporation, decisions are routinely made that affect the lives of Americans in ways that the actions of congressmen in Washington seldom do. By the hard measure of dollars, little doubt exists about the comparative importance of Detroit and Washington. In a recent peak year, 1969, the board chairman of General Motors was paid $655,000, or fifteen times the salary of a United States senator and more than three times what Americans pay their President. General Motors has $24 billion in gross annual sales (1969 figures), a sum larger than the budget of any of the fifty states or that of every nation except the United States and the Soviet Union. According to GM's records, its cumulative profit from 1947 to 1969 was $22 billion.

One reason for the corporation's gargantuan size — it has 55 per cent of the American automobile market — is that its customers keep coming back to buy its products, especially its cars, trucks, and buses available at some 13,000 GM dealerships. Many customers return because they have been conditioned to crave the chrome, horsepower, and gismos that GM puts into its vehicles. Others are the trapped victims of a corporate philosophy candidly described in April 1970 by former board chairman James M. Roche, forty-two years with GM: "Planned obsolescence, in my opinion, is another word for progress."

It is unlikely that any GM executive ever sends out memos to his staff saying things like, "Make the exhaust systems out of cheaper metal this year," or, "Order a lower-grade iron for the engine mounts." Yet in many cases he might as well, for underlings in the auto industry are quick to divine the intentions of their superiors. In February 1969, GM was obliged to notify 5.4 million owners to bring in their GM vehicles for correction of possible safety defects. Some 2.5 million of these were recalled to be checked for exhaust-system leaks. According to the Center for Auto Safety, the leaks were acknowledged by GM to have caused four deaths. One recent GM recall, in January 1972, set a national record: 6.6 million Chevrolets for possible engine-mount failure. The Department of Transportation said it knew of 500 reports of such failures. The Public Interest Research Group, a Ralph Nader organization in Washington, reported at least six deaths and a dozen persons seriously injured in resulting crashes.

Down the line of corporate responsibility, someone had thoughts about cheapening the exhausts and mounts, someone seconded those thoughts, and someone else carried them out. Death and injury resulted, and surely GM regrets it. Yet many millions of dollars of the $22-billion profit resulted also, and it is not likely that GM has regrets about that.

Consider the front bumper of the 1966 school bus, if a model in Washington, D.C., is representative. It is one-quarter-inch thick. On the 1969 model, it is one-eighth-inch thick. Thus in three years the bumper's thickness was cut in half. Considering the thousands of buses manufactured with the thinner and cheaper bumper, the savings must have been considerable. But so was and is the risk of injury and death to the thousands of school children who might be better protected with the thicker bumper.

Incredibly, as if more juice could still be squeezed from these lemons, the bumpers on these vehicles were the object of further GM cheapening. Behind the front bumper of the earlier model is a piece of steel extending from the frame in each direction about one foot, reinforcing the bumper. From the 1969 model, however, this piece of reinforcing steel is gone. And anyone who wonders why the 1969 bus rides so roughly need only measure the leaf springs that support the body. Compared to those on earlier models, the springs are seven inches shorter.

If GM cheapens parts that a layman can detect, what may it have done to parts hidden under the hood and within the chassis? General Motors, and its brother corporations such as Ford, Chrysler, American Motors, and foreign-motor companies, assure prospective buyers that they can get into their products and go tearing off at high speeds. Yet between 1966 and 1970, some thirteen million vehicles, or 38 per cent of all vehicles manufactured, were recalled for possible defects. With 55,000 persons killed by automobiles in 1971 and nearly five million injured, it is reasonable to believe that not all the carnage was caused by drunk or wild driving. Much was doubtlessly caused by defective cars, and many of those defects resulted from decisions to cut costs.

One citizen who has experienced the cheapness of a GM product is John Donovan. Unlike most owners, who have only themselves or their families to account for when they drive, Donovan has responsibility for some 250 school children, the elementary and high school students he transports to and from six private schools in the vicinity of Washington, D.C. Ever since the famous Huntsville, Alabama, crash in May 1968, when the brakes of a GM school bus failed, killing one child, Donovan has watched his vehicles closely, servicing them frequently and driving carefully. At the time of the Huntsville tragedy, he owned two GM buses, and he didn't want any injuries or deaths due to faulty equipment or anything else.

A short, broad-chested man of thirty-six, born in Oklahoma, a former Marine Corps drill sergeant, brusque in speech, John Donovan first went to Washington as a student at Georgetown University. He stayed on, married, and wound up teaching at a private school — Ascension Academy in Alexandria, Virginia. Students there describe him as a friendly, approachable man with a skill for fairness and discipline. The graduating seniors twice voted him Ascension's most popular teacher.

Donovan began in the bus business in 1963 when a neighbor in the northwest section of Washington asked him if, for a fee, he would take his child to and from Ascension every day. Donovan agreed and took out the proper commercial-carrier insurance. He soon had other requests for the same service. By the 1968-1969 school year, Donovan's business had grown; he spent $5000 to purchase a 1966 GM sixty-passenger bus and a 1959 Chevrolet thirty-seven-passenger model.

In the spring of 1969, the chance to expand still further came along, so that with more school buses he could transport 250 children. The average yearly fare was $200. Many of the children in Donovan's buses were the sons and daughters of senators, ambassadors, judges, prominent lawyers, doctors, and other important and powerful Washingtonians. Encouraged by his wife and with confidence in his capacity for hard work, Donovan decided to buy three new 1969 GMC-V-6 school buses. Each cost $8146.80. The body of this model was made by an independent company; everything else — basically, the transmission, the wheels, the engine, the electrical system, the gas tank — came from General Motors Truck and Coach Division, Pontiac, Michigan.

Early in September 1969, Donovan went to High Point, North Carolina, to pick up his three new buses. Accompanying him were two drivers, as well as a GM dealer from Laurel, Maryland, from whom Donovan was buying the

vehicles. On the return trip to Washington, Donovan had
what he called at the time "a little trouble." One bus required sixteen quarts of oil for the 300-mile trip. On the
second bus, things went fine until the accelerator spring
snapped. This meant that the driver had to put the transmission into neutral, find a place to pull over, get out, lift the
hood, and, with the engine still roaring, try to adjust the
throttle spring with a pair of pliers. The third bus worked
well until dusk, when the driver tried to switch on the head-
lights. They didn't work.

All of this irritated Donovan, but he understood that
kinks are part of a new product and no cause for alarm. Except for rattling transmissions, Donovan's buses functioned
normally for three days. He and his wife were proud of the
buses. They had risked most of their savings on them and
believed that no finer company existed than General Motors.
Donovan named the buses after his wife, Virginia, and their
daughters, Regina, who was three, and Colleen, just six
months old.

In mid-September, as required by law, Donovan took the
vehicles to be inspected before using them to carry children.
One bus passed, two did not. One rejection was caused by a
faulty brake-hose suspension. GM, Donovan believed, either
had not installed the right part or had not installed any part.
Thus, the brake hose, which is essential for stopping and
which should be suspended several inches away from the
wheel, was rubbing the wheel drag line on turns. Amazed
that a slip like this could occur, Donovan was nevertheless
grateful that the inspectors had caught it. "Thank God," he
said to his wife. "Otherwise, the rubbing eventually would
have broken the hose, and the brakes could have failed."

The second bus did not pass inspection because the exhaust-pipe hanger was faulty. It allowed the long exhaust
pipe to dangle, thereby increasing the chances of its snap-

ping. If it broke, carbon monoxide would seep out beneath the passenger compartment. "I thought the inspectors would be astonished, as I was," said Donovan, "that two brand-new General Motors buses, serviced by a GMC dealer, would fail to pass inspection. But they weren't surprised at all. They just said, 'Go get them fixed and come try again.' "

His amazement and annoyance slowly turned to dismay, for Donovan was serious about his responsibility for the lives of the children who rode his buses. Besides the Huntsville tragedy, Donovan knew of other failures of GM buses. Only the year before, eighteen children from the Accotink Academy in Springfield, Virginia, were riding in a new GM bus on Highway 236 in Annandale. The brakes failed. Somehow the driver managed to steer clear of traffic and coast the bus to a stop without an accident. The brakes were subsequently fixed three times by GM. The next year, another Accotink bus, a 1969 GM, was being driven along a highway in Fairfax County, Virginia, when the brakes failed completely. The driver steered into a pasture, and the bus lurched to a stop. *Those were new GM buses,* Donovan thought to himself, *and these three buses I just bought are new GMs, too.* His mind easily pictured one of his buses, full of children, crashing into a tree or into an oncoming car or truck. He became even more determined to do all he could to keep his three new buses in the best condition possible.

That commitment was made early in Donovan's ordeal, even though he had no way of knowing exactly what it would cost him — in loss of money, time, and peace. Between September 6 and December 6, 1969, according to Donovan's diary, he spent more than 225 hours either repairing the buses himself or hauling them to Central Motors, a GM dealership in Alexandria, Virginia. This averaged out to more than two hours daily, seven days a week. Additionally, he had to pay three of his drivers to do an extra ninety hours of repair work and hauling. A pattern emerged. When the buses finished the afternoon run about 4:30 or 5 P.M. and came to the parking lot in Washington, Donovan would ask what, if anything, had broken or malfunctioned that day. The drivers would tell him, for example, that the clutch had burned out for the second time, or that the left rear tire had leaked air for a second day, or that the bolts were falling out of the motor mounts the way they had last week, or that the wheels were wobbling, or that a gas tank was leaking, or that the power steering had failed.

The waking nightmare would now begin. Donovan would get into the broken bus and head for Central in Alexandria. Donovan's wife and two daughters would follow in the family car, so they could take him home when the bus was dropped off. It was a half-hour trip each way from Donovan's apartment in northwest Washington to Central Motors. After telling the mechanics what needed repairing, Donovan and family would return home. The girls would be fed and put to bed. He and his wife, staring at each other numbly, would have supper and wait for a call from Central — which stayed open until 2 A.M. The Donovans would wake the girls — no sitters were available at that hour — dress them, get in the car, and head for Alexandria. Donovan would pick up the repaired bus and drive it to the lot in Washington, his wife and children tailing. Donovan's records show that they made this trip approximately twenty-five times in the first three months of ownership. When two buses malfunctioned on the same day, two round trips were needed. Sometimes, since he needed to be up at 5:45 in the morning to call the drivers for the morning run, Donovan slept only three hours. During this period, both he and his wife lost weight, and friends found them unusually snappish. Donovan and his wife went out to dinner only twice in three months, and to a movie not at all.

The repairs made at Central Motors were seldom covered

by the warranty. Trying to plug the dike through which money was beginning to flood, Donovan traveled to Laurel to talk with the dealer from whom he had bought the buses. "The dealer," said Donovan, "told me my buses were obviously special cases, that these problems certainly weren't universal." Nothing could be done, said the dealer, except to notify the factory representative. Donovan called the GM public relations office in Washington and was told the man who would help him was John Nickell, the truck-and-coach field representative for that area.

Between the breakdowns of his buses, Donovan tried locating Nickell. He called several garages that were, according to the local office, on Nickell's list of places to stop. The response was always the same: Nickell either had just left or was expected at any minute. Donovan never found his man this way. Finally, in a stakeout, he went one morning to the dealer's garage in Laurel, where, the owner had said, Nickell was scheduled to appear that afternoon.

He did. Donovan, momentarily elated at talking to a live GM face, detailed the problems, from the burned-out clutches to the leaky gas tanks. According to Donovan, Nickell's reaction at this meeting, and at several to follow, was astonishment — no other operators in his area were having these troubles; therefore, aside from warranty work, GM could not be held responsible. "It must be my drivers, Nickell told me," said Donovan.

Up against a wall and wanting his conscience to be clear if any of the buses ever crashed and perhaps killed someone, Donovan wrote a letter to the parents of the children he served. "In order to facilitate safe transportation for your children with a minimum of maintenance expense," said the letter, "I purchased three new 1969 GM buses in September of 1969. It verges on the impossible to run the routes safely and on time. The reason is that these three new GM buses continue to break down. The vehicles have been fixed, refixed, and re-refixed. These malfunctions are not minor. They are major mechanical failures that often involve the safety of your children." He listed the problems and concluded: "If this pattern continues, we will have to discontinue the service."

A copy of this letter happened to come my way. I called Donovan and asked if I could examine his records and look at his buses. After several meetings in his apartment, I concluded that his complaints were valid. In any event, his anguish was real. He and his wife had put their savings into the buses, and now they appeared lost. One evening after school, Donovan asked me to take a drive with him in one of his lemons. "I'm only going to get it up to twenty miles an hour," he said, "and then I'll put on the brakes." When he applied the brakes, the bus halted with an abruptness that threw me forward. "We were only going twenty," said Donovan, opening the door and going around back. On the road were two black skid marks. The two rear wheels had locked when Donovan put on the brakes. "Can you imagine what happens," he asked, "when a bus is going fifty or sixty and the driver has to stop suddenly?"

After again looking through Donovan's material, I approached General Motors to get its side of the story and give it a chance to be heard. I tried contacting John Nickell. I left my name at his office several times, but my calls were never returned. I visited Central Motors one morning — "He'll be there all day," said a secretary in his office — but like Donovan before me, I did not find Nickell that day or any other day. Workers at Central said that Richard Lockwood, the service manager, coordinated with Nickell and that he perhaps could help me.

I approached Lockwood. He preferred not talking about Donovan's problems. "General Motors has official spokes-

men for questions from the public. You ought to ask them."
When pressed for an explanation of why so many parts on
Donovan's buses kept breaking or malfunctioning, Lockwood
said, "Some of Donovan's problems are real, some are fanci-
ful." Asked for an example of Donovan's fancy, Lockwood
recalled a visit to him by Donovan when he asserted the
clutch on one bus needed fixing. "We drove it around for a
road test," said Lockwood, "and there was nothing wrong
with it." When informed of Lockwood's statement, Donovan agreed; the mechanic did drive it around. "So I took the
bus home, with no repairs made. Maybe Lockwood was
right that time. But two days later the clutch burned out."

At 6:45 on the evening of December 9, Donovan phoned
me at home. "Guess what," he said with elation, the first
happy note I had heard from him since our initial meeting.
"GM finally knows I exist. Three of their men are coming
over to see me in an hour. They said they want to talk things
over with me about the buses. That's all they said." Donovan
asked me if I could come over and sit in on the meeting; it
might be interesting. I said that I'd be there in twenty minutes.

When I arrived, the Donovans were on the last bites of a
meal of meat loaf, canned peas, apple sauce, bread, and milk.
Their apartment, a third-floor walkup in a housing project,
was in mild disorder, a crib in the middle of the room, a chair
holding a drawer filled with Donovan's records, a filing cab-
inet in a corner, and a card table covered with invoices,
receipts, and other papers. I asked Donovan why he thought
GM wanted this meeting. "Hard to tell," he replied.
"Maybe they see my complaints are real and they finally
want to square it all up. I've heard of things like that happening."

"I haven't," cut in Virginia, "especially not from a bunch
like this. The bigger they get, the less they care." A short,

sandy-haired woman, second-generation Polish, a user of short, bright sentences, Virginia Donovan was perhaps the wearier of the two. Home all day with the girls, she had to phone parents when a bus broke down and inform them that their children would either not be picked up in the morning or be late in the afternoon. She had typed the letter to the parents as well as earlier letters to GM president Edward N. Cole, President Richard Nixon, Virginia Knauer, the Presidential consumer adviser, the Federal Trade Commission, and the National Highway Safety Bureau. She also had opened and filed the depressing form-letter replies. "It'll be a snow job, John," she said. "Just wait and see. The drifts will be so high, not even a bus could drive through."

Donovan speculated that GM had heard, probably from Richard Lockwood or someone else at Central Motors, that I was looking into the problem. "They hate bad publicity," he said. "Just the thought of a possible story in a major newspaper has flushed them out. It's funny. GM hasn't really been so bad. They've done a faithful job on the work they say is covered by the warranty. The mechanics at Central are superb. I get fast service; they're courteous. The eerie thing is that I can't find anyone who'll take responsibility for what's gone wrong."

At 7:30 the GM men arrived. Donovan, putting the infant in the crib and the three-year-old on a chair, went to the door and opened it. "Hello, Mr. Donovan," said the out-front man. "I'm Webb Madery of General Motors." Round-faced, heavy in the waist, he rubbed his hands briskly and commented on the cold outside. Madery introduced Jerry Fender and John Nickell. Donovan invited them in. The three were cheery, almost bouncy. Donovan introduced them to Virginia. Madery, with a large smile, said that he was happy finally to meet Mrs. Donovan and that everything her husband had said about her certainly seemed true. The woman did not respond to Madery's pleasantry. She knew her husband had spoken with him on the phone several times, but she also was sure her husband wouldn't have mentioned her. "What a nice little place you have here," said Madery, not letting up. He was unaware that the housewife didn't consider her apartment "nice" at all; she had told me five minutes before that her family would have moved into a house that fall if repairing the three buses had not consumed so much of their money, time, and emotions. Still icy, she took the gentlemen's coats and hung them up.

Of the trio, Madery was the oldest — sixty-two — and, as the Washington zone manager, was highest on GM's ladder. His career in the automobile industry began in 1933. After one year of college at William and Mary, he worked for International Harvester, then Chrysler. In 1958 he accepted an offer from General Motors to become heavy-duty truck manager in the Detroit zone. A year later he moved to Washington.

Fender was a trim, short-haired man of fifty-eight, with the longest GM service of the three, having begun in Oakland, California, as a twenty-four-year-old factory helper. Slowly rising from the bottom, he became shop clerk, parts manager, and so on, eventually moving to Washington as zone service and parts manager.

Nickell, forty-nine and gray-haired, had started with GM in 1940 on the assembly line in the Pontiac truck plant. He also went to school at that time, earning a B.A. in history from the Detroit Institute of Technology. Then he became a parts supervisor and began his climb.

Standing in the uncarpeted living room of the Donovan apartment and not yet down to business, the three GM men continued their cheeriness. They said they had just come from a delightful meal whose main dish was pheasant under glass. "You'd really like pheasant," said Madery to

Mrs. Donovan with an overwarm smile, apparently determined to thaw her somehow. The woman could still taste the meat loaf she had just cooked and eaten, so the news about pheasant had a contrary effect upon her.

Moving from the living room into the adjoining part of the L-shaped area, Donovan introduced the three officials to me. I stated clearly that I was a Washington *Post* writer and had begun investigating Donovan's troubles. Still engaged in the busywork of cordiality, the GM men did not seem to notice the significance of having a newsman on hand while they went about the work of customer relations. Only John Nickell, an alert, lively eyed man, looked twice at me. My name may have been familiar, perhaps from the message slips of my phone calls. Yet, after shaking hands with me at the Donovan apartment, Nickell, lowest of the three in corporate power but closest to Donovan's daily problems, seemed to let the fact of my presence pass. If his superiors weren't concerned, why should he be?

Everyone gathered around a small dining room table, everyone except Mrs. Donovan. She sat on a living room chair within hearing and took out yellow scratch paper, ready to take down in shorthand the important remarks of the conversation. The GM men produced a folder of records covering what they said was the past twelve weeks of Donovan's ownership of the three buses. As the senior official, Madery led off, explaining amiably that the reason for calling the meeting was that "GM wanted to make things right." He said that his corporation had a long record of being concerned about producing safe vehicles, especially those that carry children, and that since Donovan was concerned about safety, GM was most concerned about him. GM, he said, likes to satisfy its customers.

Impatiently Donovan broke in. "I've heard all that talk before," he said. "What I'd like from GM right now is a detailed report of the repairs you've made on my buses and also the modifications you've made on them." Donovan's request, made in a quiet but firm voice, was based on a desire to keep an accurate maintenance record. He explained that "this is the same as wanting information from your surgeon about what he cuts or takes out while operating on your insides. How can you find out unless the surgeon tells you?"

Madery laughed, saying with a final, happy grin that he had undergone operations where the surgeon never told him what he had fooled with. Donovan didn't laugh. On seeing this, Madery nodded to Nickell. "Mr. Donovan should certainly have his records," said Madery. "That's only fair." Nickell said he would get them to Donovan later that week without fail.

As the GM-Donovan case unfolded during the next year, the company never supplied Donovan the records he repeatedly asked for and GM repeatedly promised. In the week immediately after the December 9 meeting in the apartment, Donovan says, he was told by Jerry Fender that high-level officials in Detroit had made a decision not to release the records "at this time in these circumstances." The circumstances were that the first of my series of articles on Donovan and his plight had just appeared in the Washington *Post* and had been circulated by its wire service. Donovan believed GM refused to release the enormous record of repairs and replacements on the grounds that the public — specifically other owners — would learn of it and thus expect similar treatment. Donovan never learned precisely who in GM ordered the embargo. The question came up again at a meeting in January 1970 in Falls Church, Virginia, with Robert Stelter, general sales manager for the GMC Truck and Coach Division, who entered the case when it became a public issue. Donovan says he asked Stelter directly why GM had refused to release the records. Stelter, the superior of

Madery, said he himself never understood why. He directed John Nickell, also present at this meeting, to pass along the records. Nickell said he would, but he never has.

At the December 9 apartment gathering, the next topic was an itemized reading by Nickell of the repairs made at GM's expense. The list was long — including leaking oil gaskets, broken motor mounts, flawed gasoline tanks, ruptured rear-wheel seals, uneven brakes, bad tires, wobbly wheels, weak tailpipe hangers. Anyone not knowing the whole story would wonder why Donovan was complaining when GM had done all this work free of charge.

"What about those tailpipe hangers?" asked Donovan. Nickell, shooting a confident glance at his boss as if to say the question was a routine grounder and easily fielded, replied that GM had replaced them on warranty. "I know that," said Donovan, "but the replacements were of the same design as the original ones. So where does that take me?" For my benefit, and looking at me, Nickell explained in layman's terms the nature of a tailpipe hanger: a metal, straplike device hung from the frame of the bus and attached to the exhaust pipe to keep it from dragging along the road and breaking.

At this point, the smooth GM presentation showed signs, like Donovan's buses, of falling apart. The customer insisted on getting across his point that replacing a flawed hanger with another flawed hanger, however new, is not really a victory for safety. Visibly annoyed at wrangling over such a small item and apparently sensing a no-win situation, Nickell broke in to admit that "the hangers were just not strong enough. The factory made them too flimsy."

Madery looked sharply at Nickell — either startled or angered at this frank concession. He jumped in to say that studies of the hanger were already under way in Detroit and that a better one was being designed. Donovan said he was happy to hear that. He asked, however, if GM was going to warn other owners of 1969 GM buses around the country that this particular part was made "too flimsy." Madery said the decision would have to be made by higher-ups in Detroit. "I'm sure they'll tell the public," said Donovan sarcastically, "because, as you say, GM cares about its customers and the safety of children." (The flimsy tailpipe hangers have never been recalled.)

All GM cheerfulness had now evaporated. The next topic involved the leaky gasoline tanks on Donovan's buses. Nickell reminded Donovan that three weeks earlier, to show GM's good faith, he had promised to repair the leaky tanks free of charge. That was a gesture of pure largesse, Nickell made clear, because GM did not make the tank. Madery looked pleased. Nickell's statement backed up Madery's earlier one of wanting "to make things right."

"I'm not impressed," said Donovan, his anger growing. "After you told me that GM didn't make the gas tank that was leaking, I called up John Thomas [Thomas Body Company, High Point, North Carolina, the firm that had produced the bodies for Donovan's buses and fitted them onto the GM chassis]. Mr. Thomas personally told me — categorically — that his company does not make the tank, GM does."

Nickell could do nothing but admit error. Coming back fast, however, Madery explained to Donovan that, even though Nickell was wrong about the maker of the tank, it actually didn't matter, because the leak was later found by mechanics not to be in the GM-made tank but in the extension from the tank to the exterior of the bus. "That is a Thomas product," said Madery firmly. He said that GM had nothing to do with it.

Donovan could not argue further, at least not then. The next morning, however, he was on the phone again to John Thomas. I also called Thomas within the week. Thomas said, with no equivocation, that his company did not make the tank-neck extension, that it was a GM product. To be certain, I asked him to check his file and read over the phone Donovan's order page for the bus bodies; it was number 9-12202, and the facts again fitted. A few days after the apartment meeting, Donovan reported to the GM men what he had learned from Thomas. The officials, according to Donovan, "just kind of passed it off, admitting they were in 'error' again but attaching no importance to it. But I attached plenty of importance to it. I was being lied to. Not by the men who had anything to gain from the lies, but because it was corporate policy. Put me down, brush me off, keep me happy — but don't ever tell me the truth or give me new buses."

As the meeting continued, Donovan running through his list of complaints, the GM men running through their list of solutions, the question came up of whether or not these problems were limited to Donovan's buses. They had to be, said Madery; otherwise, GM would have heard from other owners. "What about Tom Gist and Billy Jubb?" asked Donovan, referring to two owners of 1969 GM school buses in nearby Maryland, with whom he had spoken at length about their mechanical and safety problems. Donovan remarked that both were experiencing difficulties similar to his own and that both said they had seen John Nickell. His memory refreshed, Nickell said that was right, he had seen Gist and Jubb. Their problems, however, were different from Donovan's, said Nickell. Once again Donovan could not refute this with absolute surety. The following day I called Thomas Gist in Sykesville, Maryland, the owner of two 1969 GMs. As was so with Donovan's buses, the power steering was bad, riding was rough, the clutches and brakes needed constant adjustment and fixing. I mentioned Donovan's name. Gist recognized it, laughingly saying they were fellow sufferers. Billy Jubb, in Pasadena, Maryland, owned four 1969s and called them "the worst I've ever owned." Each had a broken clutch. What he said about clutches echoed John Donovan: "I'm always taking the damned things to the dealer to have them adjusted."

"How does GM explain all these failures of clutches?" Donovan asked Madery. "Driver abuse," replied the GM man, starting on a brief monologue about the many ways drivers ride the clutch, pump it unnecessarily, use it wrongly. Donovan replied, again with anger, that his drivers were not heavy-footed amateurs who loved clutch-riding but were veterans of the road with at least five years' experience in driving trucks and buses. None had ever burned out a clutch on earlier-year buses. Thus, said Donovan, it was unlikely they would have ruined the clutches at the rate they were being ruined on the new buses: Two had already burned out in each of two buses; three had burned out in the third.

The talk went back and forth, Donovan repeating his concern for safe buses because children's lives were involved, Madery cordially reassuring him that GM had made things right with its warranty work and that this was a fluke problem. He had a way of feigning surprise, as if to say wordlessly to Donovan, "You're not actually saying, are you, that GM is not 'the mark of excellence'?" Not once did Madery or his two companions offer sympathy to Donovan or ever admit there might be a safety problem. If a problem was admitted, it was inevitably "not safety-related." On specific points the reply was either, "Here, this is what GM has done, so why are you complaining?" or, "Here, you should have done this, and if you had, this problem would never have happened." Nor did the GM men ever mention that their buses had been the object of recalls two years running and that this year was an extension of patterns of work developed then.

As the hour neared 10 P.M., Donovan was still spirited, but Madery, Fender, and Nickell, the taste of pheasant long gone, were tiring. As they tried to wind things down, the phone rang. Mrs. Donovan answered. "It's for you, John, from Detroit, person-to-person." Donovan took the phone and was greeted by Robert Stelter, Madery's superior. "He wants to know how things are going with my buses," Donovan remarked to the group. Answering Stelter, Donovan said the buses were just as much broken-down lemons as ever. The two talked for about five minutes, Donovan asking for his records and repeating that he worried about his brakes, clutches, gas tanks, wheels, and everything else that wouldn't stay fixed, no matter GM's diligence in repairing them.

I signaled Donovan that I would like a word with Stelter. Identifying myself and my intentions clearly, I asked Stelter how three new buses could be so flawed. The company, he replied, was doing all it could to make things right. Beyond making things right, I asked politely, would GM make things better and do as Donovan thought it should — replace the buses? The official seemed surprised that Donovan had even thought of such a solution.

After expressing curiosity about what kind of story I might be writing but careful to remain pleasant and assuring, Stelter asked to speak to Madery. As GM Detroit spoke to GM Washington, there was little but "Yes, sir" and "No, sir" from the latter. Madery concluded his conversation by saying he would call Stelter in the morning. The phone hardly back on the receiver, the GM official looked at me in astonishment: "You're a reporter?" I nodded. Nickell nodded too.

Abruptly, the GM men began putting away the materials they had spread out on the table during the evening. The phone call from Detroit, apparently meant as final proof to

Donovan that GM really cared, because his troubles had reached the ears of high powers in Detroit, had had the opposite effect. GM had learned that rather than having put down a customer, it had instead fired up a customer, one who had the crust to interest a reporter in his troubles.

Madery rose, as did Nickell and Fender, and recapturing his earlier verve, smiled broadly at Donovan and said that the evening was certainly well spent. Madery even had one last happy word for Mrs. Donovan, throwing her a compliment about "what wonderful boys" the Donovan's two baby girls were. Donovan got the men their coats and saw them to the door.

I remained for a few minutes. Mrs. Donovan said, "Let's get the snow shovels and clear out this place." Her husband saw the evening a little less bitterly. GM now knew, he said, that it could not talk its way out. "They didn't refute a fact I threw at them. That's the test. They would have slapped me down hard if one fact of mine, one record, or one document, was slightly off. But they didn't. Sure, they tried to scare me off, calm me down. What do you expect?"

After telling Donovan I would call him in a few days to check whether anything happened, I said good night.

My story of Donovan's ordeal appeared in the *Post* on December 15 and 22, 1969. On the day of the second installment, General Motors and the White House Office of Consumer Affairs held a joint press conference to announce two investigations of the 1969 buses, one by the government and the other by the company. The press conference statements of GM vice president Martin Caserio were oddly similar to the GM presentation at the Donovan apartment. Caserio said there were no complaints about the buses from other owners. Asked about the 1969 school bus that had suffered brake failure and careened into a pasture, Caserio said he believed the braking equipment on that vehicle was not the same as on Donovan's, adding, "I'm not certain about that yet." Like Madery, Caserio stressed GM's concern for safety. Thus, the faulty exhaust-pipe hanger should not be classified as a safety-related defect, because if it broke the driver could hear the exhaust pipe clattering along the ground and have repairs made before any harm was done to occupants. (But what if it merely cracked?)

Reporters pressed Caserio on Donovan's problems. For the first time the company gave a little, Caserio conceding that some of Donovan's complaints were legitimate. But always added to these admissions was the qualifier, "They are not safety-related." One reporter listed all of Donovan's problems — from brakes to clutches — and said Caserio's claiming these were nonsafety problems was an "incredible observation." The press conference did produce one memorable statement: "GM," said Caserio, "does not duck any responsibility for the finished product that bears our name."

Two months later, on February 19, 1970, a total of 4269 school buses were officially recalled by General Motors, including John Donovan's three. Also recalled were 21,681 trucks using the same model chassis. "Some of the vehicles," said the announcement, "will require installation of new brake-hose retaining springs. Some will require inspection and possible inspection and possible alignment or replacement of a rear steel brake line. A few will require both services."

At my request, GM sent me a list of forty-four owners around the country who operated more than five buses. When I called them (four people were not GM owners, and one owner couldn't be reached because he had been dead four years), I found that a recurring theme was clutch problems. One owner was a GM dealer who had so much trouble with his seven 1969s that in 1970 he bought Fords. Asked if he thought it odd for a GM dealer to buy a competitor's product, he answered, "What should I do — keep on buying buses that I know are nothing but trouble?"

Within the next year, the GM buses were recalled two more times. The second call-in involved the brakes again — possibly faulty brake-fluid reservoirs that caused the braking fluid to leak out. The third recall was for possibly flawed clutches; the clutch linkage was found to be weak— meaning, in lay terms, that the bus could lock in gear and thus be unstoppable.

Throughout the fall of 1971 and the winter of 1971, Donovan's patience held together, even though his buses clearly did not. "I began telling my wife," Donovan said, "that these buses were really unfixable. The mechanics at Central did fine work but the buses they worked on were just unable to hold up." A climax came in February 1972. The brakes on one bus were pulling and often not holding. Major repairs were done at a cost of $703. The bill was nearly a tenth of Donovan's take-home pay of $7200. The day after the brakes were fixed at this high cost, Donovan brought it to the D.C. inspection station in southeast Washington. It flunked — for brakes. If he was aghast at this, Donovan was pushed even further into the arms of disgust when the brakes flunked a second and third time — after GM had worked them over at Central Motors each time. On the fourth try, they passed.

At this sad point, Donovan finally gave up. All hope was gone that he could stay in business. With the school year closing, he drafted a letter to the parents of the children. Seek other transportation for your kids next year, he advised. "I can no longer guarantee the safety of my buses." Donovan explained that he was closing shop because he would rather have a failed business on his record than the death of children on his conscience. Before sending the letter to the parents, he gave copies to GM officials and me.

Having learned by now that Donovan could not be given a brush-off, as they had tried in 1969, an official immediately came from Detroit to Washington. "I was surprised at how prompt and courteous they were this time," said Donovan. "I imagine they didn't want me talking to any reporters, so orders may have been out to give me extra kindness." Extra kindness was indeed forthcoming. Donovan said that GM agreed to pay the $1700 he still owed for repairs during the 1971-1972 school year. Moreover, an engineer mechanic from Detroit came on to supervise repairs. With a good check-up, GM believed the buses would remain repair-free for the rest of the school year. Donovan was heartened by this attention, but not for long. From mid-March to May his buses went in for repairs twenty-two times. An official at the inspection station said that Donovan was both conscientious and wise to bring in his buses so often. "GM could give him a bill of goods," the official said, "and Donovan would never know what was what. Our tests for brakes are not difficult. Donovan's buses flunked because they could not meet even a bare minimum."

Two days after Donovan gave GM the draft of his letter calling it quits, Norman Trost, the general service manager of General Motors Truck and Coach Division, said the company was extremely concerned about its customer. "But it is very evident," he said to me in a phone interview, "that some of Mr. Donovan's complaints were due to a lack of a planned maintenance program. It's our view that he wasn't watching his buses closely. He operated them successfully for two years but then he slacked off. To prove to him that his buses could be maintained, we worked on them thoroughly and made adjustments. We wanted to get them back to a good level of maintenance." Trost acknowledged the flunks of Donovan's brakes at the inspection station, but he believed this was "just a failure of judgment at Central

Motors, not a failure of the parts. Those buses are good sound equipment and, if properly maintained, are good for many years."

Donovan was given the same message by GM, but he would have none of it. "I told them I was tired of debating. For one thing, I had my buses in twenty-two times just from March to May, so how can they say I haven't been maintaining them? I sometimes saw more of the mechanics at Central than I saw of my own kids. Either GM comes up with a satisfactory deal or I'm sending out my letter that I'm being forced out of business." A day passed. Robert Stelter asked to meet with Donovan. The customer agreed but said he would stand for neither small talk nor big talk. "I've had too much of both from General Motors," he said. In a friendly and quick meeting (there was no talk of pheasant under glass this time; in fact, Donovan says that when the GM engineers called to make an appointment, they stressed that they were calling from a Gino's hamburger stand), Stelter offered a deal. GM would give Donovan the use of three new 1972 buses for the next school year. After a year's time, Donovan could either keep the buses or turn them back to GM. "If I turn them back, GM promised me nineteen thousand, five hundred dollars for my three sixty-nine buses. In other words, they're swapping three new buses for three old ones, plus free repair work for a year. It's a good deal and a fair one." Stelter avoided the term *swap,* but said the deal was essentially a research and demonstration program. "We want to make a contribution to safety. We're trying to be fair and above board with Mr. Donovan. We want to please him and all our customers."

This reference to other customers raises questions. What if other owners of 1969 buses are as unsatisfied as John Donovan was; what about the safety of their vehicles? Apparently GM is confident Donovan's case was the exception, but I made a few phone calls and discovered that it might be otherwise. A pattern of complaint existed. A school-district official in Belleville, Illinois, said he was experiencing "the same problems" as Donovan "but we do not expect any help or cooperation from GM." An upstate New York, self-employed owner said he has had repeated brake and clutch problems. Flunking inspection is common. "It's a steady diet," he reported. "I have two Fords and I operate them at a fraction of the cost of the GMs." A rural Maryland owner complained that "I've spent as much time and money on these sixty-nines as on any other buses in thirty years of running my business." Perhaps the bitterest response was from a New Jersey owner of 1969 GM tractor-trailers who claims to have lost $200,000 in repairs, lost time, and been inconvenienced with his forty-one vehicles. "The things don't work. Almost all of mine give out after fifty thousand miles." This owner, president of a large leasing company, says he is now in the strained position of having to lease trucks from other companies — his competitors — to supply his steady customers.

John Donovan's friends jokingly call him a "giant killer," since he had taken on GM and won. "Won? How can they say that?" he asks. "Stretching it by plenty, the best you can say is that I got a tie game. I never received a cent for my lost time. They never compensated my drivers for the overtime spent in hauling the buses to the garage. They never even apologized to my wife for all those nights she spent trailing me over to Central Motors. That's the true horror of all this — not that they tried to screw one owner like me. It's the corporate callousness. Think of all the trouble they could have avoided for themselves — bad publicity — if a genuine response was made to my complaints in the beginning."

In a simpler day, a consumer with a complaint about, say,

shoes, had only to visit the local shoemaker to get justice. "Here," the customer would say, "these shoes are falling apart." The shoemaker, because he was ethical or simply aware that word would spread through the village about his sloppy work, quickly repaired the shoes or replaced them. The exchange was straightforward and there were no evasions. What's more, the shoemaker was *there,* he breathed, he had a familiar face, and the only separation between the consumer and him was his shop counter.

Things have changed. Seeking relief or redress from GM with its 750,000 employees is an agony. So it is with any large bureaucracy. The vice presidents at the top are protected from the consumers' complaints at the bottom by the mass of employees between; the latter will catch it first if the brass learns that the consumers are mad. So the vice presidents do not measure the company's success by the consumers' voice, as the shoemaker did, but by sales reports, profit charts, and the smiles of stockholders. If tens of thousands of cars are sold every year, the high-ups conclude that the public must be happy. Otherwise, why are sales up? When profits aren't up, however, or when management thinks profits can be bigger, the decision often made seems to be to cheapen the product. When such a decision can risk lives and injuries, then the ethical numbness encouraged by the profit system becomes grimly apparent.

Buck Gladden

BUCK GLADDEN HAS a third-grade education, is a $3-an-hour laborer, has a front tooth missing, and is the mayor of Anmoore, West Virginia, population 900. He is not listed among America's more courageous politicians, but to many in the dank, poor town in the black hills of Appalachia, Gladden operates on the highest levels of daring. In December 1970, to everyone's amazement and especially his own, he became the first politician in Anmoore's history to stand up to the company in the company town. And win. The victory of Buck Gladden and the five-member city council meant that the local Union Carbide factory, which consumes a third of the town's total acres and nearly all its air, was legally forced to pay its full share of taxes. A West Virginia statute authorizes an optional municipal business and occupation tax of .3 per cent on gross annual sales; but until Mayor Gladden and his council took office in 1969, no Anmoore politicians dared take the option of levying the full tax against Carbide. The law stayed on the books like a slingshot waiting for a David. Goliath Carbide, felled by Gladden, was required to pay an estimated $100,000 a year to the impoverished town, beginning in July 1971. It was not known then how much money would be coming to Anmoore because Carbide, secretive and haughty, refused to disclose its gross sales revenue. Gladden believed it would total $400,000 in three or four years, a torrential sum that would flood the town treasury as never before. Going after this haul was not a sudden surge of greed by the poor of

Anmoore. It was merely a citizen demand that Union Carbide no longer be given special treatment, because assuredly
Carbide had given the people of Anmoore no special treatment over the years.

Part of a mountain area that was long ago picked clean of
its minerals with little left behind but broken spirits and
broken backs, Anmoore is in the northwest corner of West
Virginia. The town has a harsh seeping stink that never
leaves. I could think of nothing else to ask about on enter-
ing Anmoore from a narrow mountain road and meeting
Buck Gladden outside his house. "Is that smell always
here?" Gladden repeated my question in half-mockery. He
nodded toward the chimneys of the mighty Carbide factory.
"Twenty-four hours a day," he said. "They never stop.
Production all the time for them, pollution all the time for
us." Before inviting me inside his home — a stucco bunga-
low on a hillside overlooking the Carbide operation —
Gladden offered a further comment on the tragedy of his
town. "Give me your handkerchief," he said. I handed it to
him from my coat pocket and Gladden went to a rhododen-
dron bush near the walkway. He wiped the handkerchief
on the broad face of the leaf. It came up blackened with
soot, as if the leaf were a window sill that hadn't been
washed in years. Gladden cleaned off a few more leaves, getting my handkerchief blacker, and handed it back to me.
"Want to take any more of Anmoore charm away with you?
That's what I think the name of this town comes from, the
soot. And more, and more, and more; it's just Anmoore
now."

Buck Gladden, forty-four, is large-bodied with a big
man's assurance in his walk. When he speaks, slowly and
in unvaried pitch, his wide, well-haired hands rest in a
clench. The son of an illiterate mountaineer, he made it
past the third grade but then was told by his mother that he

had to help around the house. He married at nineteen, on $23 a week. His wife was from the mountains and had neither any reason for or thought about ever leaving them. When Gladden moved with his family to Anmoore twelve years ago, he migrated from a town close enough so that he wasn't fixed in Anmoore with the dreaded label of "outsider." He took a job at the Continental Can Company in nearby Clarksburg, working the night shift as a grinder in the mold shop. If his lungs weren't filled with the dust from his grinding wheel, they were filled with the soot from the Carbide factory. At work or home, air pollution was a hazard. In the town he became known as a good-hearted man, a soft touch for the losers and beaten-down. He cared for his family, and much of his small salary went toward hospital bills because the four children were regularly stricken with lung problems. If anything set him apart from the rest of the townspeople, it was an occasional feeling of resentment at the aloofness of Union Carbide. But usually the feelings passed, pushed from mind by what others called "the realities." Like the others in Anmoore, Buck Gladden had enough in his life to fight already without taking on the company. Union Carbide was a $3-billion-a-year worldwide empire with headquarters on Park Avenue in New York and enough power to crush the uprisings of a dozen Anmoores. If there ever was to be a revolt, it would likely come elsewhere — in southern West Virginia, where Carbide operated a ferroalloy plant that nearly rivaled many urban centers in visible air pollution. To the west, a Carbide plant in Marietta, Ohio, so blackened the air with dirt that a local Catholic priest had to put a plastic encasement over the statute of St. Anthony to protect it from soot. Heavy as these clouds were, there was also the psychological one that the local Carbide managers liked to remind the people of: the company had made many gifts and contributions to the town over the years. Everyone knew of the gifts, because they were made with splashes, suggestions that no matter how troubled the social waters of Anmoore might be, Carbide had deep concern for the people.

Buck Gladden began thinking about running for mayor when attending the many town council meetings in Anmoore. In the large urban centers of America, people would rather go to the movies than to a city council meeting, but in the mountains the latter are an attraction, and possibly for much the same reason as the movies. There is a chance for laughs, possibly a little drama, but always a try at relieving the boredom. The incumbent mayor of Anmoore had held office for eighteen years. According to Gladden, "He cared more about cottoning to Carbide than he did about working for the townspeople. Some of us would get up to speak at these meetings only to be called 'out of order' or told 'to sit down and shut up.' Yet the community was impoverished — no sidewalks for the people, no playgrounds for the kids, no sewer system, no health clinic, no parks, no nothing. Not to mention the black soot everywhere, from the Carbide factory."

Intellectually, Gladden decided to run for mayor long before he made the emotional decision, the one always needed before a final action of risk is taken. His emotions were struck "one morning when I was taking my kids to school. We stopped at an intersection in the middle of the town and I saw this little girl, about six years old. She was wearing rubber boots, the kind which are worn by all the kids in our town. They have to wear them because there is no pavement, only mud and slime. The little girl was walking along, almost wading, the mud was so deep. Unexpectedly, her foot caught in the stuff, like her boot was sucked in and wouldn't come up. Trying to pull her foot free, she stepped out of the boot. She lost her balance and she had to

put her foot down in the mud, stocking and all. So she just
had to slop there. She picked up her boot and went on her
way to school. She would have to sit like that until it came
time to go home, her foot wet and slimy all morning. There
was something rotten about that, I mean a kid having to
suffer from mud. If the town had some money, the kids or
anyone else wouldn't have to walk around in the mud. They
could walk on sidewalks. That sounds strange, doesn't it?
Asking to walk on sidewalks, as though that is some kind of
impossible dream in America. But the reason Anmoore had
so much mud was that the politicians wouldn't raise the
money. They were afraid of upsetting Union Carbide —
which owed the town a lot more than a token check every
year." Gladden ran on a platform that he could do better
than that. The people believed him.

One of the first acts in Gladden's administration was to
check out the facts of Carbide's touted generosity to Anmoore. The company's presence goes back to 1901, growing from a satellite operation of the company's other and
larger plants around the country to a giant and profitable
producer of electrodes. Unlike many chemical companies,
which make products the public uses but never knows by
brand name, Carbide is visible because it markets such items
as Eveready batteries and Glad Bags. Moreover, Carbide is
an ambitious advertiser, pushing itself as the consumer's
friend and calling itself the Discovery Company. Gladden
asked the local plant manager for a list of Carbide contributions to the city over the years. "They sent me a list, in their
own good time, and sure enough, starting ten years ago, they
had been giving us things. Sometimes it was money — fifty
dollars to the school patrol one year, one thousand dollars to
city hall the next year, three hundred dollars to the little
league team, one hundred dollars for this, two hundred dollars for that. Other times, they would give the fire depart-

ment an old truck, or boots, or lanterns. All that was just fine
and we were grateful. But it was charity. It was a crumb from
the company table, things we were dependent on the management's good will to give us. The total contribution of Carbide
to the town was fourteen thousand eight hundred dollars, not
including the boots and lanterns. To get an idea how small
that sum is, just put it up against the business tax. If this
had been in effect in just nineteen seventy, the Anmoore income would have been at least six times in that one year what
Carbide's gifts were over a decade."

Having made the transition himself from suspicions about
the company to outright contempt, Gladden's political task
was to get others to make the same journey. Thus when the
time came to put the spotlight on Carbide's cheapness, the
community, not merely Gladden, would be exposing the
shadowy tactics of the company. Rousing the town was not
easy. Many believed that the almighty Carbide was a god
that would not suffer taxation graciously; it might move
away, for example, and then where would Anmoore be, with
no place to get boots and lanterns? One of those who helped
fire the daring of Anmoore was O. D. Hagedorn, a local commercial artist with an agile imagination. The first tremor
in the earthquake that shook Carbide in December 1970
came two years earlier when Hagedorn noticed an ad in a
state newspaper. It read:

A LITTLE BIT OF UNION CARBIDE IS IN EVERY HOUSE
IN WEST VIRGINIA

How true, Hagedorn recalled, a cheerful, smiling man
whose outrage is hidden by a congenial nature, "but in ways
they never meant me or anyone else to think about. The
grime and soot from Carbide's factory was not only in my
house, but in my clothes, my air, and my lungs. What a lot
of crust they had — saying they were in every house in West

Virginia." Like Gladden, Hagedorn also had his home demonstration for Carbide pollution. "Come on out to the porch and watch me sweep up the evidence," he said. Hagedorn would get a broom and a small white envelope, then sweep into it the accumulated soot particles that had wafted onto his porch. "Wouldn't it make a nice Christmas card to the plant manager?"

After Hagedorn saw the ad — and its ironic truth — he wrote to Union Carbide in New York to complain about the Anmoore pollution. A letter came back saying the local plant management would "soon" be in touch with Hagedorn. Soon never came. Traveling the same route that Gladden would later take, except that the mayor would have a measure of political power, Hagedorn moved from a position of resentment to anger. He began writing a weekly newsletter — aptly called the *Carbon Copy* — and sent it to his neighbors who were also pollution victims.

A touching example of polemic journalism, the *Carbon Copy* kept reminding the local people that they did not have to put up with the arrogance of Union Carbide, that there was a better way to live. One of Hagedorn's most successful exposures of Carbide came in an issue of *Carbon Copy* devoted to the company's Oxygen Walker. This is a nine-pound device in a portable case slung over the shoulder that provides a flow of oxygen for victims of emphysema or other chronic lung problems. Several national magazines carried double-page advertisements for the Oxygen Walker. "The gall they have," said Hagedorn one afternoon when he dropped in on Buck Gladden. "Here they are fouling and stinking the air of Anmoore and they come up with a machine to make breathing easier. Is there a better way of having it both ways than that? It's not just in Anmoore. There's the Carbide factory down in the south of West Virginia, which spews out twenty-eight thousand tons of black particles a year — a full third of New York City's annual total. I wonder how sales are in West Virginia?"

Another who wondered was the Charleston *Gazette,* the state's largest newspaper and a suspicious observer of Carbide. A *Gazette* story in late 1970 by Mary Walton, a nervy and tough reporter, told of two former Carbide workers who saw the Oxygen Walker ad. Both had heavy coughs and labored breathing, which they believed were caused by factory working conditions. They tried to get Oxygen Walkers through a local Carbide office, but no one knew about them there. The *Gazette* checked with the New York headquarters; an official reported that it was unfortunate that the Walker wasn't available in a state where lung problems were common and where the company had its largest operations. According to the *Gazette,* he hoped a distribution network could soon be set up, but the hilly terrain of West Virginia posed problems: "It's hard for a distributor to run the thing and make a buck."

When Gladden ran on a platform of taxing Carbide, the town rallied behind him. The candidate promised that, if elected, he would take the option of levying the municipal business and occupation tax of .3 per cent on Carbide's gross annual sales. After winning by a close margin (198 votes to 139) — some in the town feared the waves that inevitably come when boat rockers appear — Gladden took after Carbide. In addition to Hagedorn, he was joined in his pursuit by two young lawyers, Larry Silverman and Willie Osborn, members of Ralph Nader's staff in Washington; they had been living in the mountains for six months for the sole purpose of gathering facts about the operations, public and private, of Union Carbide. The pair came to Anmoore and, after going through the short tunnel of suspicion which all outsiders in Appalachia must pass, were warmly accepted by Gladden. The lawyers researched the complex legal questions involved, to be sure that when the challenge to Carbide came it would have no legal loopholes for the corporation to slip through.

On the evening of December 3, 1970, in the town hall packed to a capacity of seventy-five, Gladden struck. "No more special treatment for Carbide," he said. "From now on, they're just another taxpayer in the town." Most people in the assembly cheered. One man who didn't was A. J. Dornseif, the local Carbide plant manager. Earlier in the day, I phoned the corporation's headquarters in New York for its view of Mayor Gladden and his tax. Declining comment on the mayor, they spoke about the levy: "Our argument is that we should be fairly taxed, but not beyond the budget needs of the city. There hasn't been the proper examination of the Anmoore budget needs before this tax was passed. We think the city council may have acted hastily." Dornseif repeated this view, ending with a plea to the gathering of townspeople that they be sensible about this whole thing and make sure they know their budget needs. Before Mayor Gladden could answer this, Margaret Golden, a councilwoman and one of the three members elected on the Gladden slate, stood up, enraged. "We know our budget needs only too well, Mr. Plant Manager. Just walk through this town. The mud is everywhere. We have no sewer system so the cesspools overflow into the streets. Our kids walk in it. We have no parks, no health clinic, no children's playground. All of this, and then the soot is everywhere. Thanks to you. How can Carbide ask us to examine our budget needs? What needs examining around here is the conscience of Union Carbide."

Dornseif, not put off and realizing that the vice presidents in New York would want a report on the meeting, rose to remind the council that his company already was paying about 90 per cent of Anmoore's tax revenue, mainly through the real property assessment. Mayor Gladden agreed, but remarked, "Your assessment is only thirty per cent of your property's appraised value. Everyone else is assessed at fifty per cent."

After the meeting, Gladden, Hagedorn, and Silverman were elated. The mayor, not a public man and relieved to have this tension behind him, excused himself. "I got to be up early in the morning — take my kids to school and be off to my job, my paying job, I mean." Silverman and Hagedorn stayed around to talk. "We didn't come in and create this defiance," Silverman told me. "It was already here, in Buck and the others. If we made any contribution, it was merely to provide a kind of cement by which the townspeople could put together their energies. We have nothing against Carbide, no spite, no anger. I'm even a stockholder. Carbide makes many fine products. My main concern is to see that the laws on the West Virginia books are applied as equally to the company as to anyone else in Anmoore." Hagedorn, who called the evening the most historic in the town's history, had sympathy for Dornseif. "I feel for the local management," he said. "They aren't responsible for the soot that blackens this town. They take orders from someone higher up and in turn he takes orders from someone higher than he. Finally, you get to the top man — Birny Mason, the board chairman. But he's so occupied with the total corporate picture — pleasing the stockholders, making decisions about plants in South America, Africa, Asia, all over the U.S. — well, how can he even think about the dirty air in Anmoore?"

Actually, Mr. Mason, or at least his aides, are thinking about the problem. At the time of the Anmoore uprising, this thinking took two forms. Publicly, officials pointed proudly to a document called "Summary of Union Carbide's Program for Pollution Control." This tells about the firm's

progress in attacking air pollution, citing the $47 million
that will eventually be spent to bring its three factories in
or near West Virginia into compliance with the latest laws.
What isn't mentioned in the glow of this report are the many
years that Carbide has resisted federal urgings to clean up
its mess. The details have been reported nationally many
times. In early 1967, a conference was called, by law, to discuss an abatement schedule at the Carbide plant in Marietta,
Ohio, across the river from Vienna and Parkersburg, West
Virginia. "But Carbide avoided our requests for information about the factory's emissions," an HEW compliance
man said later. "They wouldn't even let us in the factory to
look around." In October 1969, another conference was
held, but Carbide boycotted it. Recommendations were
made, however, and accepted by HEW in April 1970; these
called for a 40 per cent reduction in sulfur-dioxide emissions by October 1970. Two months after the deadline, Carbide wrote to the new Environmental Protection Agency
proposing only a 12.5 per cent cut and that by December
1971. When EPA responded negatively, Carbide, playing
one of its more wornout aces, said that it might have to lay
off 625 workers in order to comply. This form of environmental blackmail was also heard in Anmoore the night the
tax was levied. Dornseif hinted to the gathering that if the
town played rough with Carbide, then Carbide might have
to play rough with the town — by pulling up and moving
elsewhere.

After the meeting, I had a short word with Dornseif, as he
flew off, head down. "It's these outsiders," he said, nodding
to Silverman and Osborn, "who cause the trouble." The next
morning, I asked Buck Gladden about the "outsider" issue. The mayor agreed with Dornseif, with a twist he found
grimly amusing. "The outsiders definitely are the problem," he said. "The Carbide plant in Anmoore has nine

hundred workers, but only forty of them are from Anmoore, less than five per cent of our population. And none of them are in executive jobs. So it's true, the outsiders are causing the trouble."

Two years after he won his first term and a year after he taxed Carbide, Gladden came up for reelection. In a campaign described by O. D. Hagedorn as "incredibly bitter," Gladden's opponent was the previous do-nothing mayor; the latter, wired like an Eveready to the cross-currents of Carbide, said in a campaign letter that the tax was "the most unfair he had ever seen." The community didn't think so. On election day Gladden had 170 votes, the ex-mayor 120.

"During the campaign," the two-term mayor recalled, "a few people who didn't like me — they worked for Carbide — saw me on the street one day. 'You're no politician,' they told me. I thanked them for the compliment. It's when I do become a politician that I'll start to worry. Meanwhile, we're getting some sidewalks built in Anmoore, a playground is going up, and the streets are being paved. And it's been six months since I've seen one of our kids fall in the mud."

Posey Stewart

DEAD MEN TELL no tales, the saying goes, but often the way they died tells the story well enough. Deep in the mountains of southern West Virginia, the way life ended for a fifty-two-year-old coal miner named Posey Stewart says much about coalfield poverty, the philosophy of the leaders of the United Mine Workers Union and the attitude of some of the nation's largest corporations. The public mostly hears about coal miners when they are killed in high-carnage mine blasts, like Farmington, West Virginia, which took seventy-eight lives in 1968, or the one in Hyden, Kentucky, in 1969, resulting in thirty-eight corpses. But these stories are usually reruns of an old tragedy, repeat performances that have killed more than 100,000 men since 1900. The events that led to the needless death of Posey Stewart were different and had a grim kind of freshness; his sufferings are still alive among thousands of miners and their families who are trapped in pits of despair as lethal as any doomed mineshaft.

I learned of Stewart's life during a visit to the West Virginia mountains and became curious about the stories miners and their wives were telling about their fallen friend. They spoke with reverence. Stewart had done what many of them wanted to but wouldn't: get out of line. By luck, the facts of Stewart's final ordeal were documented in legal records held by Harry Huge, a Washington public-interest attorney in the mostly private-interest law firm of Arnold and Porter. Huge, who helped in the trials that led to the conviction of UMW president W. A. (Tony) Boyle, be-

lieves the mountains are filled with potential Stewarts waiting only for a break in the political weather before they
come out.

Born in 1918 in Clear Fork, West Virginia, the son of a
coal worker, Stewart went into the mines at the age of fifteen.
He worked as a tippleman, one who dumps coal from a huge
ramp into waiting railroad cars. After a few years, he shifted
jobs to become a driver of the small motorized cars which
go into the blackness of the mines to bring coal to the surface. The job is risky due to the dangers of cave-ins and of
having one's head bashed in or ripped off by hanging rocks
or timber pilings.

Stewart drove for twenty-four years. Like every miner in
Appalachia, he well knew that the ceiling and walls of the
shaft were his enemy, able to give way and crush him without notice. In 1947, while looping his way through the mo-
torcar trails of the No. 2 mine of the Eastern Gas and Fuel
Company, Kopperston, West Virginia, the enemy struck.
Stewart, pulled free of the rockfall, suffered a broken back
and crushed ribs. As tough as the mineral he mined, he recovered and, amazingly, returned to the same mine to do
the same work. He made it untouched for a few years, until another rock-fall accident. Forty-six years old, his spine
buckled and his lungs almost gone from breathing coal dust
for thirty-one years, with a heart attack on top of it all, Stewart never mined again.

As a loyal and dues-paying member of the United Mine
Workers of America, and a beneficiary of the union's Welfare and Retirement Fund, Stewart's hospital bills from his
two accidents were paid for; he carried the hospital card of
the Welfare and Retirement Fund, and that covered expenses. One of the hitches regarding the treasured hospital
card is that fund regulations permit a miner to hold it only
while employed or pensioned. From some 50,000 men who

have not yet reached the retirement age of fifty-five — and who can't work because their bodies have been crushed or maimed — and men who are over fifty-five but have not qualified for a pension, the fund stops paying the medical bills after one year. Stewart felt this was a betrayal. He gave two thirds of his life to the coal companies and the UMW; they, in bitter return, offered him nothing when he most needed everything. He was forty-six, with a family, and had only social-security pennies to survive. He said to friends: "I told the fund people that I may not make it to age fifty-five, when I could get my miner's pension. I asked them, what am I going to do in the meantime?"

United Mine Workers is the nation's most powerful union; the electric-power utilities ride on its decisions and America rides on electricity. The coal business is booming again — 590 million tons was the projected tonnage for 1971, the highest total since 1947. With the country's gluttonous appetite for electricity — everything from electric toothbrushes to electric subway cars — only more and more can satisfy the hunger. Posey Stewart remembered the early days of the union, when organizers would come into a coal camp with "fire in their bellies and a light in their eyes. We would follow them anywhere. Now those men are old, and all they say is 'Don't do that, don't cause trouble, don't disturb things.' Thirty years ago, they were saying, 'Do it, shut down the mines until they make the mines safe, and pay us a decent wage, and give us our union.' " That was tens of thousands of deaths and injuries ago; the situation today was described in a *Fortune* magazine piece where Monseigneur Charles Owen Rice said: "The union that once protected the men from the bosses has become the union that protects the bosses from the men."

Stewart, getting no help from the UMW and not surprised that he didn't, became a leader in a group of wheezing, gimpy disabled miners and miners' widows. The original purpose of the organization was vague, a refusal to be slapped down, a try at "getting what is rightfully ours." Within two years, however, after another group of workers closed many of the highest-producing mines and forced the West Virginia legislature in early 1969 to pass a black-lung compensation bill, Stewart's organization knew exactly what it wanted. In the summer of 1969, they sued the UMW and the Welfare and Retirement Fund to regain their hospital card and pensions.

Little came of this move, and still less after Joseph Yablonski was murdered; fear came to the coalfields. Once it passed, however, a group of Yablonski supporters formed Miners for Democracy. Led by a neighbor of Stewart's — a disabled black miner, Robert Payne, who had suffered three amputated fingers and a scarred back — it went beyond lawsuits. In July 1970, Payne called for a strike in the mines of southern West Virginia, asking that the workers boycott the pits until the fund gave the miners their due.

Stewart never joined Miners for Democracy, on the advice of Harry Huge, but Stewart was seen one afternoon talking to striking miners on a picket line. From informers, the coal companies mistakenly heard that Stewart was one of the leaders of the wildcat strike that began cutting production and profits. In August of that summer, Stewart suffered his fourth heart attack. His wife answered the phone one day, her husband in bed, and was told by an anonymous voice that it would do Posey "no good to get well, because I'll kill him as soon as I see him." Mrs. Stewart, though frightened, was able to ask why. "Because of those strikes."

More chilling than this call, which could be seen though not passed off as the work of a lunatic, was Stewart's ordeal in the four weeks between the strike he didn't join and the heart attack he didn't want. Some of the nation's largest coal

operators — including U.S. Steel and Consolidation Coal
Company (the Farmington people) — had obtained court
orders against Stewart, along with several other crippled and
old miners. This was not the project of a crazed night caller, but the reasoned plan of board-room officials. The companies claimed that Stewart, a man with a crushed spine, almost no lungs, and three heart attacks, posed a threat to
the nation's security and, more locally, to the economic well-
being of the coal industry. The legal action of the coal companies aimed at having Stewart's moves stopped immediately
— because the picketing was spreading and mines were being closed across the West Virginia coalfields.

Marshals continued serving papers during the day and
night at the Stewart home in Oceana, bringing the legal documents that "commanded" the broken man "under threat
of law" to appear in federal district courts in Bluefield and
Charleston. Always the knocks came loudly and suddenly,
always from marshals who were sullen and curt. Each time,
Stewart took the papers in disbelief. "What have I done?"
he asked his wife wearily. A trusting man with a mountain
instinct for fairness, Stewart thought his defense would be
easy. He was not a striker, hadn't been, and wouldn't be.
Huge, although he had been up against the corporations
before, could do nothing in this case but advise Stewart to
appear in court and answer questions.

So began a two-week legal nightmare. Some of the most
twisting and trickiest roads in the nation wind over and
around the mountains between Oceana and Bluefield. Driving in his own car at his own expense and his own time, Stewart had to rise at 4 A.M. each day to make it to the courtroom
in time. The first two days, Stewart might as well have
stayed home. He received no call to testify. He sat idle in a
small witness room off the chamber of the hearing room.
Awed by the mighty surroundings of the court complex and

frightened at the close-up power of the coal-company lawyers who would soon be at him, Stewart sweated through the
first two days. On the third day — again, one that began
at 4 A.M. — Stewart was called to the witness stand. Repeatedly, the lawyers asked him why he picketed the mines.

"I didn't picket the mines," Stewart answered.

"Who did you picket with?" they returned.

"I didn't picket with anybody because I wasn't there."

It continued all morning. Threatened with jail if he
"kept picketing," the pressure and tension increased while
Stewart kept telling the judge and the lawyers that he had
never begun picketing. "It's getting to me," he told Huge as
the hearings wound on. "Why are they hounding me? I told
them I didn't picket. They just seem determined to get me,
one way or the other."

Each night, after the hard cross-mountain ride home, Stewart slumped into a chair exhausted. He complained to his
wife that the ordeal was too much. "I'm innocent and
they're not listening. They keep asking me the same questions. It's as if they want to wear me down." Stewart could
not spend long hours in the comfort of evening conversation
with his wife. He had to rise the next morning at four to return for more possible testimony. Each of the fifteen coal
companies involved in the hearings were entitled to call on
him, even though each well knew what he had said to the
lawyers of the other companies.

When Stewart left the courthouse in Bluefield on his last
day of testimony, he said he needed a rest, that his
body couldn't take any more. It didn't. He soon had the
fourth heart attack. Because Stewart had no money and no
hospital card, his doctor had to fight to get him admitted to
the hospital. He stayed a week, though he needed intensive
care for at least thirty days. He came home and died within
ten days. The charges against Stewart were immediately
dropped. Now that he was dead.

PART II

Paths of Spirituality

Dorothy Day

"THE BEST TIME to come up would be anytime," Dorothy Day said over the phone when I asked to come visit her. The time was early summer in 1966. I had been working in the New York bureau of United Press International as the twenty-fifth man in their twenty-five-man sports department. Unsportingly, management decided it could send out the scores and game details with twenty-four men, so I was dropped after three months, just when I had learned both the names of the people I work with and all the big league baseball teams. Dorothy Day and those with her in the Catholic Worker movement owned a farm overlooking the Hudson, about two hours upriver from New York City. I wanted only to spend the afternoon, though Miss Day said I was welcome to stay a week, a month, whatever.

I wanted to talk with this saintly and heroic woman and perhaps use the compass of her wisdom to get a direction on where my life ought to go. A few years earlier, I had met Dorothy Day when she visited the Holy Spirit Monastery, a Trappist community in rural Conyers, Georgia. I was there from 1960 to 1966, trying out the life, but leaving before making a permanent commitment. Miss Day spoke for about an hour, in a low-ceilinged room with hardwood benches, telling the fathers and brothers about how she began working among the poor in the 1920s, her hospitality house in the Bowery of New York, the college students who worked summers among the wrecked people that she cared for, some of those who had helped put out the *Catholic Worker* news-

paper — Michael Harrington, Ammon Hennacy, Thomas
Merton, John Cogley, Tom Cornell, Nicole D'Entremont,
Jack English. Unlike most visitors to Trappist monasteries,
Dorothy was neither awed nor mystified by it all.

"Don't forget," she said, "you're supposed to be poor.
Give away what you don't need. Get by on essentials.
Wealth hurts monasteries more than anything else. The
contemplative life can't be lived the same time you're living
the comfortable life." From anyone else, this kind of hard
talk would have been sent back over the net in a swift volley
of indignation. But it was accepted, even cherished; Dorothy
Day had lived in voluntary poverty all her adult life, so she
could speak about it not as a concept but as an experience.

On the afternoon of my visit, the farm at Tivoli was
crowded with people. Some were sick alcoholics who had
come up from the Bowery to dry out. Others were young
conscientious objectors, new believers in the kind of pacifism
that Dorothy Day had been teaching for thirty-five years.
A few were misshapen people whose souls had been bent by
illness or poverty, with no hope of recovery but at least a
chance at being comforted. Nearly everyone had a responsibility at the farm, perhaps baking the bread, or going into
town for the mail, cleaning the floors, tending the vegetables,
mailing the newspaper. Some were too ill to work, or too
confused, but room was made for them nevertheless. A large
number of those who came to the farm were young idealists,
full of zeal and full of eagerness, but not role players because
Dorothy was an unwilling audience for showoffs.

I recalled that in Georgia she had spoken about the young
who come to work at the House of Hospitality or the farm,
all moved by an energy that wants to do good but often none
of them having the slightest idea how to apply it. "Sometimes
it seems that the more volunteers there are around the place,
the less gets done," she said. "I have letters from six volun-

teers on my desk now. Not only are all the beds full, so that
we cannot put them up for the Chrystie Street work, but also,
it seems in regard to these we already have that their interest in peace keeps them from the clothes room, or from the
paperwork connected with thirty or more subscriptions coming in each day . . . Paperwork, cleaning the house, cooking
the meals, dealing with the countless visitors who come
through all the day, answering the phone, keeping patience
and acting intelligently, which is to find meaning in all these
encounters — these things too are the work of peace, and
often they seem like a very little way."

I met Dorothy as she walked across the lawn before the
main house. A degree or two had been added to her stoop
in the three years since I had seen her. She suffered from
arthritis, something her friends say was caused by too many
years sleeping without blankets after putting them over
derelicts taken in for the night. Her hair was yellow-white,
braided over the top the way it was when Dwight Macdonald
wrote the memorable *New Yorker* profile in 1956. She had
soft brown eyes in square-cut sockets. Her body didn't fill
her dress, which rustled in the easy breeze and always stayed
mussed. She wore no stockings and her shoes were black
and functional, the kind nuns wore before relevance got to
them.

She remembered her visit to Conyers, and said with
amusement that the Trappists were good to talk to because
they were a sure audience, as captive as any. She asked after
Brother Charles, an old friend who had run a hospitality
house for vagrants in Cleveland for a few years but then
joined the Trappists. We talked about the large numbers of
people who were leaving the religious orders. Dorothy saw
it as an eruption of hope and not a signal for worry. Many
were realizing at last that Christianity was not a religion for
specialists. She said she had seen, and liked, a long article

I had written earlier that year for the *Critic* magazine on this same point, and believed the Church should be glad, not upset, that so many were leaving. They might be getting out of the structural Church but there was no abandonment of the Christian ideals. For some twenty minutes, we talked about the farm, some of the conferences to be held that summer and fall at Tivoli and about the cross-country trip Dorothy would be taking soon. Without my asking, Dorothy suggested that I keep up with my writing, even though at the moment I had no job or much of an outlet. A lot of things, she said, were not being written, especially about the lives of the poor. We get plenty of news stories on the poverty program and the issue of poverty, but not many writers go out to look at how the poor are suffering. That needs to be told, she insisted, otherwise who will know the poor are there? Nothing is easier to get adjusted to than other people's misery.

We had been sitting on the stoop of the porch, and from behind someone called Dorothy to the phone, a long-distance call. I waited five minutes. Grateful for the time she had already given me, I decided it would be bad manners to consume any more. I walked around the farm and about an hour later, from a distance, saw Dorothy driving off to the train station. We waved.

When I wrote a short essay not long ago on Dorothy Day on the editorial page of the Washington *Post,* I guessed that few of my fellow workers would know much about her. For one thing, many of those who came out of the Catholic Worker movement, or at least read about it and occasionally sent in a small sum — I was in this group, a reader and sender — tended to be possessive of Dorothy. She was *our* heroine, *our* saint, not for the talk shows, much less to be in the secular hive as anyone's queen bee of wisdom. Amazingly, on the day the piece appeared, at least six reporters in the busy sprawl of the *Post* newsroom stopped me to talk about Dorothy. These were newsmen on national beats, men of tough curiosities who had low toleration of causes and whose cynicism about the world's good-doers was crusted by years of reporting the let-downs and failures of this goodness. Nor were they especially religious men — though men of solid ethics, which is even better — and certainly not churchy. Yet each had a private story about Dorothy Day, some recollection of her immense achievement and how they once, sometimes often, had brushed close to her courage on some past reporting assignment.

Radicalism is now a cheapened word, at high pitch and low level, mocked by showmen from Eldridge Cleaver to Jerry Rubin and the other sophomores who think that social upheaval produces social improvement. But no better radicalism exists than the kind practiced by Dorothy Day — the wild extreme notion that Christianity is a workable system, the bizarre idea that religion has more to do with what you work at than what you believe. "It is a strange vocation," she recalled not long ago, "to love the destitute and dissolute, those people sleeping in doorways, foul with the filth of the gutter, dying of drunkenness and malnutrition, fever and cold. We have known many such deaths on Chrystie Street and have witnessed the depths of misery around us. Only last month, a group of school children, early teen-agers, poured kerosene on three such men, sleeping in a doorway, and set fire to them. This act of horror gives witness to the all too prevalent attitude to these men. 'They are only bums,' one child said; and the mother of another, 'Someone ought to do something about these bums.' Yet they are found in every corner of the city, in vacant buildings, in the shadow of warehouses in neighborhoods deserted at night."

Caring about ideals that reasonable men long ago gave up as lost, Dorothy Day easily seems out of touch to the follow-

ers of today's causes. When the women's liberation movement first picked up steam in the summer of 1970, Dorothy
addressed a conference at a college in Westchester, New
York. Betty Friedan and her howitzer manner was there,
gunning everyone down, guilty of oppressing women or not.
A black sister read an absurd bitch manifesto. Then Dorothy
Day spoke. A report in *Commonweal* magazine described
her as "perhaps the oldest person in the room, the most personally courageous, and in action and practice, already the
most liberated." Miss Day "said nothing about women's
liberation, never mentioned the words, never stated her
views on the subject of economic equality, careers, chores,
society's institutions. Instead, she reminisced about her life,
her daughter, the families she has known, the poor, the work
she'd done, in jail, in the streets, in her houses of hospitality."
It was the unwritten text she spoke from when visiting the
Trappists in Georgia, minus the call to poverty.

As with most vocations that stay singular in purpose over
long periods of time, Dorothy Day came to hers the long way
around. In her early twenties, she lived on the cheap as a reporter in New York. She liked the work, but the itch for action competed with the job of reporting the action. With an
unbribed heart that sought out the rich experiences where
self-identity is created automatically as one goes along, her
circle included Malcolm Cowley, John Dos Passos, Allen Tate,
and Caroline Gordon, all starting out then in Greenwich
Village. One of Dorothy Day's fondest memories is the evenings spent in the back room of a Fourth Street saloon where
Eugene O'Neill would recite for her "The Hound of
Heaven." Moved by this poem of faith, and by longing that
could not be satisfied by conventional activism, she eventually
embraced Christianity. With a child from a common-law
marriage — over quickly — she met in 1932 Peter Maurin.
He came on easy with a hard message, a drifting reformer al-

ways bobbing up at the scenes of injustice to tell people how
to build a "society in which it is easier for people to be good."
Together with Dorothy Day, he founded the *Catholic Worker*
newspaper. In its pages for the last thirty-eight years, it has
been like a prowling animal outside the doors of America's
deaf and lazy institutions. Danilo Dolci, the Berrigans,
Jacques Maritain, Thomas Merton, Martin Buber, Gordon
Zahn have written for its pages. In the introduction to a valuable collection of articles from the *Worker — A Penny a
Copy, Readings from the Catholic Worker,* edited by Thomas
C. Cornell and James H. Forest and published by Macmillan
— the editors write "that some would like to consign this volume to the racks as a memento to the thirties. Let it be a
thorn in the side of our parents. But that cannot be. For it is
still going on, and to tell the truth the misery is deeper and
the frustration more bitter, the apocalypse closer and each
present moment more acute. Wars and rumors of war, race
war, class war. Wars of liberation and wars to liberate the liberated. And as always the same victims. The people. The
vast majority of the people, poor and hungry, sick unto death
of liberators, whose cry is 'peace and bread.' The Body of
Christ bleeding from a billion wounds. And still the Catholic
Worker movement, poor among the poor, a quiet leaven,
a bowl of soup, an oddly dated monthly, still a penny a copy,
bringing news that is so old it looks like new."

Many of the war resisters who have served in prison, now
served, or who have left the country rather than bear arms,
first learned about pacifism and civil disobedience (but not
civil destruction) from reading Dorothy Day or going to her
meetings in the Bowery. A recent article in the *Catholic Worker* — all articles there are "recent" — noted that
"the young men working here are conscientiously opposed to
war. Perhaps after having seen the victims of the class war
in this country sleeping forgotten on the Bowery, running up

and down the steps of crumbling tenements, or staring wide-eyed and alone in mental hospitals, they do not want to fight for a materialistic system that cripples so many of its citizens . . . These are young men who have learned well one historical fact — that you can never win over an ideology by killing the men who have the idea. The job at hand is that of a peacemaker performing the works of mercy, not the works of wars."

One reason so many professional journalists know Dorothy Day is because her newspaper is an exceptional achievement. Easily, it is the only paper in the country to have kept so long to one editorial line, to one typographical tradition, and to one price. In paying homage to this rarity, Dwight Macdonald wrote in the introduction to a collection of *Catholic Workers*, each given in its entirety, published in 1970 by the Greenwood Reprint Corporation: "The thirty-sixth anniversary issue of the *Catholic Worker* — May 1969, Vol. XXXVII, No. 1 — looks, reads, and costs the same as that of May 1, 1933, Vol. I, No. 1. Only the *New York Times,* another of our few stable institutions though its editorial line is jittery compared to the *Worker's,* has a longer typographical tradition (by some thirty years). Unlike the *Times,* the *Worker* costs the same now as it did in 1933: a penny a copy, 25 cents a year — the only periodical in journalistic history that costs twice as much by the year as by the issue." When Macdonald's piece was excerpted in the *New York Review of Books,* the editors footnoted it with the customary "it appears here by permission of the publisher and the author." They went on to add: "The volumes included in this edition are 1 through 27, 1933 to 1961. The price will be $435.00. If a foresighted collector had bought these numbers on the street and stashed them away, he would have paid $3.48 for the lot (29 years at 12¢). A considerable saving — $431.52, to be exact." On the newspaper itself, Miss

Day recalled that the first issue run in May 1933 "was 2500 copies. Within three or four months the circulation bounded to 25,000, and it was cheaper to bring it out as an eight-page tabloid on newsprint rather than the smaller-sized edition on better paper we had started with. By the end of the year we had a circulation of 100,000 and by 1936 it was 150,000. It was certainly a mushroom growth. It was not only that some parishes subscribed for the paper all over the country in bundles of 500 or more. Zealous young people took the paper out in the streets and sold it, and when they could not sell it even at one cent a copy, they gave free copies and left them in streetcars, buses, barber shops, dentists' and doctors' offices. We got letters from all parts of the country from people who said they had picked up the paper on trains, in rooming houses. One letter came from the state of Sonora in Mexico and we read with amazement that the reader had tossed in an uncomfortable bed on a hot night until he got up to turn over the mattress and under it found a copy of the *Catholic Worker*. A miner found a copy five miles underground in an old mine that stretched out under the Atlantic Ocean off Nova Scotia. A seminarian said that he had sent out his shoes to be half-soled in Rome and they came back to him wrapped in a copy of the *Catholic Worker*. These letters thrilled and inspired the young people who came to help . . ."

A typical issue of the paper, which can be subscribed to at 36 East First Street, New York, New York 10003, usually has a woodcut on page one, often a scene of oppression or perhaps a depiction of a hero. Carried in the eight pages will be a report from one or two sites of injustice — a migrant labor camp, perhaps, or maybe a hospital ward in a city "health" center — an appeal for winter clothing, an easygoing column by an old-time member — Deane Mary Mowrer's "A Farm with a View," written from the Catholic Worker farm in Tivoli — a news story about an editor being arrested for refusing military induction (how many of these stories there have been), a couple of book reviews — and always the important books, too, such as Gordon Zahn's *War, Conscience and Dissent,* or Danilo Dolci's *The Man Who Plays Alone* — a long essay or two on nonviolence or welfare reform, a lively "Letters to the Editor" column (lively not because nutty letters are printed, but because such nutty ideas as peace, sharing the wealth, serving the sick, reforming the government are discussed and debated) column-end fillers — something from Bernanos perhaps, or Solzhenitsyn, often *Tales of the Hasidim* — and always Miss Day's column "On Pilgrimage."

"I am home again with a handful of colorful postals," she wrote after returning from her trip to Russia during the summer of 1971, "including reproductions of ikons and a folder of picture postals of Lenin's exile in Siberia, where he lived, where he studied, where he taught his peasant neighbors and their children, where he fished and hunted and rested in the forest. How I wish we had such a Siberia where the Fathers Berrigan and all the prisoners of conscience could go and meditate and study and prepare for a new social order 'wherein peace and justice dwell.' "

Dorothy Day's autobiography is *The Long Loneliness,* a treasure in the tradition of Augustine's *Confessions* or Merton's *Seven Storey Mountain.* It is a moving book, the classic story of someone seeking a piece of earth of which to be the salt. The prose is clear, unpretentious, and conversational, much the way Miss Day is in daily relationships. A humility is present in her style of writing soldered together with the humility in her own life. Repeatedly, she refers to Charles Peguy, Ignazio Silone, Eric Gill, Piotr Kropotkin. The thoughts of these men are not abruptly plunked into Miss Day's text like fall-out from Bartlett's, in the manner of hack politicians wanting the eloquent sound. Instead, attracted by the play of ideas, Miss Day delights in passing on the genius of others, a servant of truth who gladly carries the tray that holds the treasures of others. Among those she leans on are William James. Tellingly, she included in her autobiography: "One afternoon as I sat on the beach, I read a book of James' essays and came on these lines: 'Poverty is indeed the strenuous life — without brass bands or uniforms or hysteric popular applause or lies or circumlocutions; and when one sees the way in which wealth-getting enters as an ideal into the very bone and marrow of our generation, one wonders whether the revival of the belief that poverty is a worthy religious vocation may not be the transformation of military courage, and the spiritual reform which our time stands most in need of.

" 'Among us English-speaking peoples especially do the praises of poverty need once more to be boldly sung. We have grown literally afraid to be poor. We despise anyone who elects to be poor in order to simplify and save his inner life. If he does not join the general scramble, we deem him spiritless and lacking in ambition. We have lost the power even of imagining what the ancient realization of poverty could have meant; the liberation from material attachments, the unbought soul, the manlier indifference, the paying our way by what we are and not by what we have, the right to fling away our life at any moment irresponsibly . . .' "

How willingly poor has Dorothy Day lived? One example might be from a quiet event in 1960 when she sent back a large sum of money to the treasurer of the city of New York. The letter tells much about the soul and the beliefs of Dorothy Day and her refusal to adjust. "Dear Sir," she wrote. "We are returning to you a check for $3579.39 which represents interest on the $68,700 which we were awarded by the city as payment for the property at 223 Chrystie Street which we owned and lived in for almost ten years, and used as a community for the poor. We did not voluntarily give up the property — it was taken from us by right of eminent domain for the extension of the subway which the city deemed necessary. We had to wait almost a year and a half for the money owed us, although the city permitted us to receive two thirds of the assessed valuation of the property in advance so that we could relocate. Property owning having been made impossible for us by city regulations, we are now renting and continuing our work.

"We are returning the interest on the money we have received because we don't believe in 'money lending' at interest. As Catholics, we are acquainted with the early teaching of the Church. All the early councils forbade it and in various decrees ordered that profit so obtained was to be restored. In the Christian emphasis on the duty of charity, we are commanded to lend gratuitously, to give freely, even in the case of confiscation, as in our own case — not to resist but to accept cheerfully.

"We do not believe in the profit system, and so we cannot take profit or interest on our money. People who take a materialistic view of human service wish to make a profit but we are trying to do our duty by our service without wages to our brothers Jesus commanded in the Gospel (Matt. 25). Loaning money at interest is deemed by one Franciscan as the principal scourge of civilization. Eric Gill, the English artist and writer, calls usury and war the two great problems of our time. Since we have dealt with these problems in every issue of *The Catholic Worker* since 1933 — man's freedom, war and peace, man and the state, man and his work — and since Scripture says that the love of money is the root of all evil, we are taking this opportunity to live in practice of this belief, and make a gesture of overcoming that love of money by returning to you the interest.

"Insofar as our money paid for services for the common

good, and aid to the poor, we should be very happy to allow
you to use not only our money without interest, but also our
work, the works of mercy which we all perform here at the
headquarters of *The Catholic Worker* without other salary
or recompense than our daily food and lodging, clothes, and
incidental expenses. Insofar as the use of our money paid
for the time being for salaries for judges who have condemned us and others to jail, and for the politicians who ap-
pointed them, and for prisons, and the execution chamber
at Sing Sing, and for the executioner's salary we can only
protest the use of our money and turn with utter horror from
taking interest on it. Please be assured that we are not judg-
ing individuals, but are trying to make a judgment on the
system under which we live and with which we admit that
we ourselves compromise daily in many small ways, but which
we try and wish to withdraw from as much as possible."

Unlike many who care for the poor and other discards of
our system, Dorothy Day has not merely given until it hurts,
she has given until after it hurts. She owns nothing herself,
knowing that the teaching of voluntary poverty is a sham if
one does not also live it. Had she been less austere on herself over the years — not sleeping in cold rooms, eating on the
run, traveling on Greyhound buses — perhaps the physical
hurt of old age would also be less. But what is a little thorn
in the side? she asked once. "It seems to me we might begin
to equal a little bit of the courage of the Communists. One of
the ways my American Communist friends taunt me is by
saying, in effect: 'People who are religious believe in ever-
lasting life, and yet look how cowardly they are. And we
who believe only in this life, see how hard we work and how
much we sacrifice.' "

Despite bishops and priests who condone war and lead the
government at prayer time, Dorothy Day has never judged
such men or left the institutional Church. It is probably be-

cause she is still loyal to this rich and highly organized body that she can say: "Why worry about empty schools, seminars and even rectories? Maybe the Lord is giving us a little reminder that there has been too much building going on, and that it is time to use some of these facilities for the poor, for families." In a column entitled "Meditation on the Death of the Rosenbergs," she expressed what many have felt on seeing Cardinal Spellman troop off "to be with the boys" or when Cardinal Cooke shows up at a White House prayer service to be court chaplain to Richard Nixon: "What a confusion we have gotten into when Christian prelates sprinkle holy water on scrap metal, to be used for obliteration bombing, and name bombers for the Holy Innocents, for Our Lady of Mercy; who bless a man about to press a button which releases death to fifty thousand human beings, including little babies, children, the sick, the aged, the innocent as well as the guilty."

Valuing communal living long before communes came into fashion, Dorothy Day has always had farms in the country for her companions. Tivoli, New York, is the current site, overlooking the Hudson River and complete with vegetable gardens and flowers. No stranger has ever been turned away, much less old friends. The lonely and confused come back loaded with problems, to retreat awhile and talk with Dorothy. She feeds them first, like Jesus and the five thousand. And in the winter at Christmas in the Bowery, the strays who come to her get a little wine with the meal. Why not? They are human beings, in need of joy and mercy, like everyone else.

Thomas Merton

A FEW WEEKS BEFORE he died by a fluke accident in December 1968 in Bangkok at fifty-three, Thomas Merton wrote a circular letter to his friends. One copy came my way. The woman who sent it said she was surprised, even dismayed, that the world's best-known Trappist had left his monastery in Kentucky for a long leave of absence. "Leave of absence?" she asked; how can that be? Merton, she thought, was in "for life," and now here he was out of his monastery, running around and having a jazzy time like the rest of us.

To this lady, and to many other people, Thomas Merton had become over the years the symbol of Trappist life and its severe routine of stability, silence, and seclusion. It was reassuring to know that Merton and the other fathers and brothers at Gethsemani, Kentucky, had cut themselves off from secular diversions and were attending to the true realities of life, the spiritual kind. Oddly, many of those who marveled at how the Trappists could lead such devoted and spiritual lives were themselves actually living heroic lives: fathers and mothers serious about the vocation of marriage and raising children, or professionals, like lawyers and doctors, who put the poor's interest before their own. In many ways, the sacrifices demanded of these people were greater than the ones of Trappists.

Merton refused to be a symbol, even worse, a fantasy symbol. On reading his easygoing letter — written from New Delhi — it struck me that he was only doing for a few months in Asia what he had done for twenty-seven years in his mon-

astery, six years at Columbia University, and a stretch at a
settlement house in Harlem: seeking God and serving men.
More specifically, Merton was in Asia because he had long
studied and loved Tibetan Buddhism and Japanese Zen.
Down the years, he had received many invitations from Tibetan and Zen masters to visit their monasteries and become
an exchange monk because he had much to teach and much
to learn. But Merton's abbot refused to let him go, saying outside contacts were not a part of the contemplative life. Other
reasons were present also. It would have been disaster, from
the abbot's point of view, to let Merton out the gate, and then
see the brilliant and gifted artist turn up in places like Milwaukee to march with Father Groppi, in Catonsville to be
jailed with the Berrigans, in Los Angeles to do God knows
what with Sister Corita. Merton would be more headlined
than all four combined — not because of any particular protestant skills but because he would register out of Trappist,
Kentucky. The public would delight in following the city
capers of the monk whose image was largely built on solitude
and silence. Back home, Gethsemani without Merton would
be just another struggling religious house, about as promi-
nent as Mt. Michael in Elkhorn, Nebraska, or Daylesford
Priory, Paoli, Pennsylvania. It would take Merton about a
week to write his first life-in-the-city book — "The Seven
Storey Tenement" — and another week for every American
Trappist to read it; the same crowd who piled in on a Merton
book would now go out on a Merton book.

To keep any of this from happening, Merton's superiors
kept him under special wraps. Unlike many other Trappists
who regularly shuttled around from one monastery to another to teach, help out at harvest time, or merely take a vacation, Merton was never allowed to visit another Trappist
community. He had received many invitations down the
years. Nor did his superiors ever let him attend a general

chapter, the annual meeting of Trappist abbots to exchange ideas on what the order is and what it should be. The given reason for excluding Merton was always, well, this is an abbots-only meeting and Merton is not an abbot, so what can we do? As a result of being denied a position of leadership (a daughter house of Gethsemani reportedly elected Merton their abbot, but his own abbot at Gethsemani denied the request), Merton gradually lost interest in membership. For a few years, he had been living apart from the community in a hermitage on the outer reach of Gethsemani's property.

The man most responsible for making Thomas Merton into Gethsemani's most important product was his abbot, Dom James Fox. A believer in strict discipline, the kind that would make a Marine boot camp look like Burning Tree Golf Club, Abbot Fox came from the same style of Catholicism that produced Cardinal McIntyre in Los Angeles and Cardinal Spellman in New York. His motto was, "All For Jesus, with a Smile." But concerning Merton's thinking for the last ten years of his life, Abbot Fox had little to smile about. The obedient Merton, who once produced safe devotionals on the silent life, the living bread, the ascent to truth, and so on, suddenly became what the *National Catholic Reporter* called "the public monk." He openly and accurately exposed the shallowness of his Church, order, and government. That he passionately loved all three and hoped his thoughts would help open the way for new policies made no difference. It wasn't the kind of thinking to keep up an image and, perhaps more serious, it was questioning the style of monasticism that Abbot Fox had spent a long career building up.

Early in 1968, old age forced Abbot Fox to retire, whereupon his successor gave Merton the green light he wanted. In the Himalayas, the Trappist spent eight days with the

Dalai Lama. "We spoke almost entirely about life and meditation," wrote Merton to his friends, "about samadhi — concentration — which is the first stage of meditative discipline and where one systematically clarifies and recollects his mind." About Tibetan monks in general, Merton said, "They are specialists in meditation and contemplation. This is what appeals to me most. It is invaluable to have direct contact with people who have really put in a lifetime of hard work in training their minds and liberating themselves from passion and illusion."

As a man who did exactly that himself, Tom Merton — what he liked to be called, rather than his monastic name of Father Louis — found that he was living both a deeply private spiritual life while also leading a public life through his writing. Since the middle 1940s, his thoughts on men and God were expressed in a steady flow of books, articles, poems, and letters. Editors found him a soft touch, which meant that you were always coming upon his pieces in obscure journals like the *Downside Review, Jubilee,* and Dorothy Day's *Catholic Worker,* as well as the popular magazines like *Saturday Review.* The widest read of his more than thirty books was *Seven Storey Mountain,* his autobiography written in 1949. Toward the end of life, Merton hinted privately that perhaps it would have been better had he held off writing it until he was further into the spiritual life. He knew, with sadness, that the book drew hundreds of young men into the Trappists who had no real taste or insight for the monastic style of spirituality. And worse, some spent twenty or thirty years in the monastery only to find they were really ducking life, not seeking God.

The years I spent in the Trappists, in the Holy Spirit Monastery, Conyers, Georgia, were from 1960 to 1966. Although Merton never visited Conyers — it was the first off-shoot of his community in Kentucky — his thinking, even the spirit of his presence was deeply felt. Occasionally, one of the fathers or brothers from Conyers would need to go to Gethsemani, sometimes on business, other times for a break from the routine, sometimes to get help from the priest-psychiatrist who was a member of the community there. Invariably, one of the thoughts of Merton that would be carried back was one that brought great peace to many in our small community: don't be afraid of leaving the monastery, or worry about feeling guilty afterward. People have temporary vocations, Merton believed. This is one of the functions of the monastery — to be a type of graduate school where instead of working on a thesis, you can work on yourself. If you have vocation to the life, good; if not, that's all right too. You were generous to come and spend a few years trying it out. In the end, whether you work out your salvation here or out in society, what should be remembered is this — you don't have a vocation, you are a vocation.

In religious orders today, an idea like that is now a basic assumption. But ten or fifteen years ago in the Trappists, an order that in many ways hadn't changed its style in 700 years, it was brash thinking. Impressionable novices in some of the twelve American monasteries could easily tremble about the thought of leaving. The traditional teaching was that once you came, you stayed. In the *Little Flowers of St. Francis of Assisi* an early chapter is titled "How St. Francis Appeared in Glory to a Novice Who Was Tempted to Leave the Order." Naturally, St. Francis put some sense into the youngster's head; the story ended when he "came back to himself. And encouraged by the vision of St. Francis, the novice rejected all temptation and acknowledged his fault before the guardian and the other friars. Henceforth, moreover, he longed for the roughness of penance and of the habit as for wealth. And thus converted into a better man, he lived a very holy life and died in the Order." Franciscan superiors

no doubt relied on that anecdote to persuade their newcomers to stick it out, but Trappist superiors had a better story (though the progressive abbots never used it). One
day, a young man who had been in the monastery a few years
decided his time was up, that he ought to leave and try something else. But it's God's will that you stay here, his abbot
told him. Sorry, said the young man, I'm going; this is a fine
place and a great life but it's not for me. On the day he left,
the young man walked into the nearby town to get transportation back home. Ten minutes out the front gate, a car ran
into him. He was hospitalized for six months and spent the
rest of his life paralyzed in bed. The pious ending to
the story is the old abbot's remark to that evening's chapter
meeting: "Fathers and brothers, the novice should have
stayed. God got him anyway."

I don't know how many men were kept in the Trappists by
this particular story (at my monastery, a relaxed place, the
story was told with a different ending — the abbot runs out
the gate with a lasso trying to recapture the ex-novice and he,
the abbot, is run over), but the moral is sound: don't trifle
with the Lord's will. The thinking of Merton — that leaving the monastery can be as much in accord with Providence
as staying — came at the right moment for me, when I was
already in the Trappist community four years, with one
year to go before the rule required a decision to take solemn
vows for life or leave. It was like being engaged to be married
for four years and then having to decide whether you actually should or shouldn't marry. I decided not to. I would
have left the monastery whether I knew of Tom Merton's
thinking or not, but knowing it made the going a positive experience, and let me feel proud that I had given five years
to the Trappists. No cars hit me when I walked out the
gate and into Conyers; in fact, the abbot himself, a kindly,
generous man, drove me to the Atlanta airport. He handed

me three hundred dollars and bought my plane ticket to New York — one way.

When I received the circular letter from Merton in Bangkok, I recalled his notion of temporary vocation and how apparently he was now applying it to himself. Many have since debated whether Merton was in the East permanently or only on a private work-release program. The question didn't matter to me at the time, mostly because I was elated to see Merton physically in the Orient because he had been there so often spiritually. More important, it suggested that even after twenty-seven years in his monastery, Merton had kept alive a spirit of healthy nonadjustment. Constantly walking in lines — from and to the chapel, the refectory, to the work fields — he nevertheless refused to get in line with the image that many people, including Trappists, insisted that Trappists project: silent, obedient fellows away from the world and its errors.

A year before he was killed, I wrote him at Gethsemani, explaining that I was preparing a long article on the Trappists for the *National Catholic Reporter*. At that time, the *Reporter* was one of the liveliest weeklies in the country and one which did much to generate the reform movement in the Catholic left. I asked Merton if he had any thoughts he might want to contribute. In kindness, he wrote back a fair-sized letter, one that struck me then, and even more so now, as an example of how a person can adjust to enormous severity — the Trappist daily life — yet refuse adjustment to those parts of the life that have been cheapened or distorted.

His letter, echoing some of the articles he had been writing in the mid and late 1960s on the present troubles and future prospects of monasticism, was pointedly concerned about the individual's survival in a large organization, regardless of how noble the organization's goals. The styles of some of the

African monasteries were hopeful, he believed, as were those
of the Little Brothers of Jesus, an order founded by Charles
de Foucald, the saintly missionary to a nomad tribe in the
northern Sahara who once had spent seven years in a Trappist
monastery. The famous Protestant monastery of Taize,
France, also had some enlightened leaders. As for American
monasteries, Merton was less hopeful. Some were doomed to
complete inertia while others — his own included — were
stumbling along, eager to find a way but unsure of a direction. The organizational approach, guaranteeing an institutional image, was mistakenly being favored. This implied no
decadence; instead, it meant being stuck in the gear of neu-
trality, overly concerned about the Order's established position, its comfortable prosperity. After Vatican II, a few
monasteries were quick to make changes in the vernacular
liturgy that they saw as revolutionary, but barely two years
passed before the changes were seen as merely routine. The
challenge is to make the contemplative life not more toler-
able but more meaningful, and this was the failure of the
monastic institutions. Men and women came to seek meaningful and creative lives but found only a routine style of
living being offered. Small wonder many looked elsewhere
after a few years. One of the specific misfortunes of established monasticism, Merton said, in America and elsewhere,
is its thousand-year identification with *milieu Catholicism,* a
phrase of Carl Amery's, a German theologian. When a choice
must be made between the spirit of the Gospel and the demands of a Church too close to a social and cultural order, the
latter, the milieu, easily wins. Sanctity, even prophecy, is
still possible but the institution has so lost touch with the importance of these qualities that it sees them as strange or foreign, either to be suppressed or absorbed. Merton believed
a genuine ferment was going on in the monasteries (something
I discovered to be true in researching articles I eventually

wrote on the Trappists for the *National Catholic Reporter*
and the Washington *Post*). He insisted that the issue was not
one of making the life softer or increasing its relevance, whatever that was, but of the Order coming to some kind of agreement on basic values. He resented the idea that the term
contemplative life was being used defensively to keep the
fathers and brothers in the monastery, to cut them off from
the world's suffering and needs, to silence the dialogue with
the community. In his own way, meaning no ill will to his
superiors, much less a backing off from his vows, Merton
said he was living on the margin of life at Gethsemani. He
mentioned, without bitterness, the rejection of his requests
for permission to travel, adding wryly that such requests
produced almost catatonic shock in his superiors' minds. The
letter closed with words of friendship.

Looking back through the articles and books that Merton
produced at about the time of his letter to me, it is uncanny
that he was writing in the mid 1960s what many are only getting around to now. In February 1972, for example, a dozen
towns along Buffalo Creek in southern West Virginia were
washed away by a flash flood from wastes of a coal mine
owned by a large corporation, the Pittston Company. One
hundred twenty-five were killed and some 4000 left homeless.
Four years before, perhaps with the gift of prophecy that he
often talked about, Merton wrote: "Much of the stupendous
ecological damage that has been done in the last fifty years
is completely irreversible. Industry and the military, especially in America, are firmly set on policies that make further
damage inevitable. There are plenty of people who are aware
of the need for 'something to be done': but consider the
enormous struggle that has to be waged, for instance in eastern Kentucky, to keep mining interests from completing the
ruin of an area that is already a ghastly monument to human
greed. When flash floods pull down the side of a mountain

and drown a dozen wretched little towns in mud, everyone will agree that it's too bad the strip-miners peeled off the tops of the mountains with bulldozers. But when a choice has to be made, it is almost invariably made in the way that brings a quick return on somebody's investment — and a permanent disaster for everybody else."

On Vietnam he wrote, a year before Nixon came to power: "We intend to go on bombing, burning, killing, bulldozing and moving people around while the numbers of plague victims begins to mount sharply and while the 'civilization' we have brought becomes more and more rotten. The people of South Vietnam believe that we are supporting a government of wealthy parasites they do not and cannot trust . . . We are getting to the point where American 'victory' in Vietnam is becoming a word without any possible meaning."

Many of Merton's friends in the secular and intellectual worlds thought it only a matter of time before their liberal and energetic friend would wise up, leave his monastery and priesthood permanently, and get where the action was. Whether he would have done this is now a question which, like Merton, is dead. It is true, as the letter shows, he often felt confined. But not by the walls of the monastery nor even by his abbot. He felt confined because he couldn't grow enough — grow more in the love of God, grow more in the service of his fellows. Just as he knew that wheel-spinning was the main activity of many doers and reformers, he knew also that "solitude is not withdrawal from ordinary life . . . On the contrary, solitude is the very ground of the ordinary life. It is the very ground of that simple, unpretentious, full human activity by which we quietly earn our daily living and share our experiences with a few intimate friends."

My own guess is no, Tom Merton would not have left his priesthood or monastery. In a time after his circular letter, he had planned to take leave of Asia, and his Buddhist and

Zen brothers, and return to his Trappist brothers in the Kentucky monastery. Because, he would say smilingly, the action was really *there*.

PART III
Remembering Children

Mitch Kurman

WHAT IS WORSE for parents than the death of a child? One thing only — when the death is needless and could have been avoided. No parent, whether a Vietnamese mother whose child was killed by American bombing or an American father whose son was killed because of corporate negligence, ever fully recovers. Interior peace, the most valuable kind, is forever gone. One reaction to losing a child needlessly is to push the event from the mind, send it trackless into the inner space of memory where it will remain forever but at least be traveling in a random orbit away from the soul. Bury the dead and let life go on. Another reaction — more rare, more heroic — is to keep the tragedy fresh and current by alerting others that the conditions by which your child was killed still exist. Other children may die needlessly, perhaps yours. This is the vocation of the lantern — lighting it, going out into the darkness of unconcern and apathy, trying to focus on a major national tragedy but illuminating only small corners, not whole rooms. Who listens? Who cares?

A letter came in November 1971 from a Westport, Connecticut, furniture salesman named Mitch Kurman. Handwritten, in sprawling script, he asked if I would consider writing an editorial for the Washington *Post* supporting legislation for a youth summer-camp safety bill. The Senate, Kurman's letter explained, had already passed a bill with a unanimous vote of 53-0. The House would soon be debating similar legislation, choosing between a bill that was much stronger than the Senate version and a bill much weaker.

Kurman's letter ended by saying that a *Post* editorial on summer-camp safety would be timely and possibly helpful. Letters asking for editorial support are common but usually they come from a politician — senator or congressman — who has sponsored a particular bill, from a trade association whose interest is totally vested, sometimes from a lobbyist looking out for a client. Here's our bandwagon, the letters commonly say, just hop on, we're going places. I have never written a piece solely on what a letter says or urges, because a fair part of a newsman's salary is for him to be suspicious. Kurman's letter had to be treated this way also, but it was clearly different from most of the others. It was from a private citizen, on plain stationery, and about legislation that obviously could be of no financial or political benefit to him.

A few days later, after researching the history of summer-camp legislation, speaking with four or five Senate and House staff people, and talking with my editor, the *Post* ran an editorial. It supported the bill of a New Jersey Democrat, Dominick Daniels, that called for strong safety standards for summer youth camps. These minimum federal standards could then be administered by the states; the latter would receive up to 80 per cent funding from the federal government to administer them. The Daniels bill, presented as a new title of the Higher Education Act, was an effective approach because it provided incentives to let states run their own programs while insuring that nationwide standards would be met. Thus, a camp in one state would have the same minimum standards as a camp a mile across a state line or a camp 2000 miles across the country.

Many children are sent to safe, well-run camps where supervision is firm and accident prevention is taken seriously. This is not true for all children, however; many are at camps where counselors have little knowledge of dangerous waters or trails, where safety equipment is not provided, where safety and health inspections are rare or nonexistent. The statistical breakdown between safe and unsafe camps is not known. A possible guide is that out of 11,000 camps in the country, only 3500 are accredited by the American Camping Association, and even then the A.C.A.'s inspections are not strict. Only twenty-six states have legislation concerning sanitation. About fifteen have safety regulations that would be meaningful. Only three or four make reference to personnel. Over the years, Congress had passed all kinds of bills to protect alligators, coyotes, birds, and bobcats, but it was not yet concerned about the 250,000 children annually disabled from camp accidents. A week later, the House debated the youth camp-safety bills. It rejected the Daniels proposal and in its place approved an amendment offered by Representative J. J. (Jake) Pickle, a Texas Democrat. This called for a survey of the situation. Three Congresses — the 90th, 91st and 92nd — had held hearings on summer-camp safety, taking testimony from dozens of informed witnesses; but Pickle thought more study was needed and, incredibly, the House agreed. Taking a survey is a favorite Congressional stall, a mañana maneuver that delays and confuses.

For the *Post,* the backing of another defeated bill meant little. We took the stand we thought was right, but in the end the defeat of the Daniels bill was only another mark in the won-lost columns. In the weeks after, though, I kept wondering about Mitch Kurman. Was the defeat only a passing event for him? Did he go on, as we did, and take up other issues, shelving camp safety until it would come up in a future Congress? The questions bothered me, so I phoned Kurman and asked if I could visit him in Westport. He seemed surprised — "I usually have to go to the press, instead of the press coming to me" — but we arranged a date convenient to both of us.

Mitch Kurman, forty-eight, the grandson of Jewish immi-

grants and the father of two daughters, is a furniture-manu-
facturers' representative. He knows what the factories are
making and what the stores are selling, and puts himself in
the middle. The work takes Kurman throughout New England and down the East Coast as far as North Carolina. Self-
employed, his office is in his basement; both his wife, Betty,
and his father help on the paperwork. Although Westport
has the image of a fashionable and smart-set community, the
Kurmans live in an unsplashy neighborhood, a few blocks
off the Merritt Parkway. Kurman is short, gentle-speaking,
and totally gracious. His life since August 5, 1965, has been
one of lonely nonadjustment, a vigilance that has tried to
disturb the peace that calmly allows 250,000 children to be
injured every year and large numbers killed.*

   "My son David was drowned in a canoeing accident in
Maine that August," said Kurman, seated on the living room
sofa. "I am not a wealthy man but I am not pleading poverty either. I guess you might say I am a man of possibly
better-than-average means. I did not want David growing
up in a goldfish bowl of Westport. I thought it would be
good for him to get around. The boy loved to read. He was
a fine student and I thought it would be good for him to go
off to a camp and learn something about the outdoors. The
camp we sent him to was in New York State, run by a YMCA
in Rochester. The camp sent us a brochure which I think
would satisfy anyone had they looked at it and studied it. I
certainly had the utmost confidence in the boy's ability to
swim and I certainly did not expect anything like a drowning. I expected adventure. I expected fun. I expected good,
hard work, and I expected him to be paddling, which is

---

* Statistics on camp fatalities are hard to come by. In 1965, the Mutual Security Life Insurance Company of Fort Wayne, Indiana, made a study of 3.5
million campers, mostly children in organized camps. Between the years 1962
and 1964, 88 death claims were submitted.

what I wanted and which is why I sent him there. I did not send him on any expeditionary situation, something to endanger his life."

On August 5, the YMCA group made its way to the west branch of the Penobscot River near Millinocket in Maine. The campers were going down a section of the river called Passamaquoddy Falls when a number of the canoes were overturned by the rough waters and jutting rocks. The YMCA counselor had not supplied the boys with life jackets. "When David was killed," Kurman said, "it took a three-and-a-half-day search to find the boy's body. The waters the group tried to pass through was a raging hellhole that no man in his right mind would ever attempt. I graduated from Cornell as a biologist and if I was ever told to investigate that water, I would probably sit on a riverbank and write out a report. I would not go into that water. When I went up to look at the waters myself, I learned that the Great Northern Paper Company has a large paper mill in the area. They shoot their cords of pulpwood logs to the mill downriver and in this stretch where David was killed, the logs actually tumble end over end."

Kurman speaks emotionally about the negligence of the YMCA and it is hard not to suspect that perhaps he exaggerates; after all, it is an unsettling subject. On checking the record, however, Kurman, if anything understates the situation. In a trial held in district court in New York in May 1971 — the case took six years to reach a judge — Kurman won a settlement of $30,000 from the insurance company of the YMCA in Rochester. Among those testifying were the chief of police in Millinocket, a deputy sheriff, and two of the boys on the trip. The police chief testified that the canoes used by the YMCA were unsuitable for the rivers because they had keels, good only for placid waters, not rapids. The sheriff testified that the YMCA counselors, intent on making time, would not participate in a search for the Kurman boy after the canoe overturned. Instead, the paper company closed down its operations and sent out special search parties to find the boy. In his suit against the YMCA, Kurman charged that the leaders of the trip were inexperienced, had selected waters which were dangerous for canoeing, had no life jackets for the boys, and no ropes or snubbing poles to guide the canoes away from the rocks. The defense called no witnesses. Kurman recalls the irony of the phone call from the YMCA following the accident. "They told me — bluntly and coldly right over the phone — that David drowned because he disobeyed instructions."

Shortly after the accident, Kurman made the first of what would, in six years, be hundreds of journeys to get legislation for camp safety. "Maybe I just should have forgotten about the whole thing," he said. "People tell me I'm a little crazy for keeping with this tragedy all these years, since nineteen sixty-five, with no letup. They mean well and they tell me to relax, forget about the past. They ask me how I don't go out of my mind to fight this. The facts are the opposite, though. I'd lose my mind if I knew these conditions existed and didn't do anything. A friend of mine, a kind guy, says maybe a psychiatrist could help me forget about David and about camp safety. He means well, but isn't it strange? I don't need a psychiatrist. I'm normal. My friend needs the help. He looks away from the reality."

The first trip after the accident that Kurman made was to the office of New York Governor Nelson Rockefeller. "I was naive. I thought if you brought this to the attention of the officials they would do something, they would tighten up on the situation so it wouldn't happen again. I certainly did not expect to see my own boy alive again, but I felt why should this happen to someone else's child? I brought it to their attention and I asked them if they could tighten up to prevent similar tragedies that might happen with other children sent to camps in New York State. I was told, 'Well, what do you expect us to do?' I said, 'There must be some legislation. There's a law for spitting on the sidewalk. There ought to be a law for taking care of the camps for children.' They told me, the people in Rockefeller's office, that the camps in New York have to comply with the sanitary code. I asked what that meant and they said that it simply means safe food and safe water. I asked, 'What about personnel?' and I was told they were not concerned with personnel. So I asked how you are going to determine if a camp is safe when you want to send a child to one. I was told, 'They print brochures, that's how you tell.' I was amazed that they said that, because the next summer after David was killed, the camp issued the same brochure it had sent me a year earlier."

The experience with Rockefeller's people jolted Kurman. Moreover, this particular issue involved kids — keeping them safe. Who would not be for that? Kurman was soon to find out.

Because his furniture work took him to about a dozen state capitals, Kurman was able to get to the politicians. He also went to the newspapers, television and radio stations to get their support. (Kurman has a file weighing more than 100 pounds, filled with clippings from the New England and national press.) The media rallied behind him, with a few exceptions. As for the politicians, they also were for camp safety, at least while Kurman sat before them explaining the problem. "Sure they were," he said. "Here I am in their office, telling them about my boy who drowned, what else can they say?" Yet saying and doing are not the same, and Kurman discovered in New York what was to become a long agony of consensus solutions. He found an assemblyman in Albany who sponsored a law calling for life preservers while in pleasure boats. "It was a mild bill," said Kurman, "just requiring that people strap up in a life preserver when they took to the water. It passed the assembly a hundred forty-seven to three. But on its final reading the bill was starred. This is a technical term meaning that the legislation is temporarily dead until the star is removed. I begged the majority leader of the assembly to remove the star — because he had the power to do so — but he declined. So the bill died.

"I kept at it. In the next session, I spent at least one hundred hours lobbying for the bill — personal visits to Albany, to Niagara Falls to see a state senator, to Utica to see an assemblyman, to Astoria, Queens, to see another assemblyman. This time the bill passed, Rockefeller signed it, and I said to myself, well, the system will work if you just keep at it. But I was astonished to find that in the final version of the bill an exemption was made — for private ponds and lakes, exactly the waters where most of the summer camps are located. So there was really no law at all, as far as I could see. In fact, the law that was passed was worse than no law at all, because now parents would be fooled and think their kids were protected at camp." Kurman has never been able to find out who slipped the exemption through.

When he went to work on the Connecticut legislature, known as a fickle group, Kurman found that the editorial support of the state's newspapers — from the small and conservative Greenwich *Time* to the large Hartford *Courant* — had already alerted the politicians. Grimly, something else also aided the chances for a life-preserver law. While the bill was being debated in committee, five teen-age boys in Fairfield County took a small sailboat into Long Island Sound in rough waters. Only two life jackets were on board. The boat capsized, with three boys drowning and two surviving. The latter had on the life jackets. Although the politicians, moved by this tragedy which was felt throughout the state, quickly passed the law, Kurman noticed there was still pressure to weaken it. Several groups, representing camp operators, were involved. Kurman wrote to the state's Department of Agriculture and Natural Resources in Hartford and found a sympathetic official in Bernard W. Chalecki, director of the Boating Commission. Chalecki replied that when the law went into effect many requests were received from the Boy Scout camps asking for exemptions. The Boy Scouts said they could not afford to buy a sufficient number of life-saving devices, so the law should not apply to them. The Boating Commission never granted the exemptions. An irony of the Boy Scout request is an article from a Boy Scout magazine titled "Trip Fun with Safety." "Life vests or jackets should be standard equipment for every canoe trip — one for every person in the party. These life vests are to be put on and worn by every person on all occasions when conditions of weather or water indicate there is any possibility of danger of upset or swamping from wind, waves, rapids or other causes. They are to be put on before the danger area or time is reached and kept on until after the time of hazard has passed . . ."

Kurman's eye easily saw the sparks of contradiction flying off this flinty opposition. "There are the Boy Scouts — holy, pure and all-American, preaching safety for the public to behold but all the while trying to get around the law in quiet." The Boy Scout evasiveness has not been confined to Connecticut. They have been at work in Texas also. State Senator Lane Denton from Waco wrote to Kurman in March 1971 that a youth camp-safety bill had been introduced by him in the Texas legislature and sent to a subcommittee. Even at that early stage, Denton said, "the main opposition was from the Boy Scouts and the private camp operators." With wit, Denton added that since these two groups were opposed, "this type of legislation is definitely needed." Four months

later, Denton wrote to Kurman with the bleak news that his
bill had died in subcommittee. "The Boy Scouts led the fight
against the bill," Denton said. It would be eighteen months
before the Texas legislature would again meet.

At the same time Kurman was going after the state politicians, he was also coming to Washington. A national bill was
his goal. In six years, he believes he has seen every senator
(or every senator's legislative assistant) and nearly all the
representatives. One of those on the Hill visited by Kurman
in the early days and who has stayed with him since is Dan
Krivit, chief counsel for the House Select Subcommittee on
Labor. His subcommittee was the pad from which a youth
camp-safety bill would be launched, if at all. "I remember
when Kurman first came around," Krivit recalled. "He was
emotional. He did all the talking. He made demands.
He damned congressmen as do-nothing politicians. God, he
came on strong. But I have a rule — that you have to distinguish between the guy who has facts and the guy who has
bluster. You can tell soon enough. We see a lot of special-
interest people who are mostly big talk with small arguments. The appeal of Kurman was that he had a command
of the facts. I was able to check them out pretty quickly and
see that he was right."

Another whom Kurman saw in his early trips to Congress
was Representative Dominick Daniels of New Jersey. A
kindly man who works hard but one of the anonymous herd
of low-profile congressman, Daniels took an interest in Kurman and agreed to hold hearings. In July 1968, he told his
colleagues on the opening day of testimony: "This morning
we take the first major step forward to provide minimum
federal safety standards for summer camps across the nation.
We must identify the nature and magnitude of such problems as may exist, and consider whether state and local regulations are adequate to deal with them. If we determine

during the course of these hearings that a significant problem exists, I pledge that I will do everything in my power to ameliorate the situation. Summer camps deal in what is perhaps the most precious commodity we have — the lives of our youngsters."

Although the hearings were a success and glowing statements of support were heard for the Daniels bill, nothing ever came of them in the way of legislation. Dan Krivit said that "we couldn't muster enough enthusiasm." Kurman was dismayed that Congress did not act, particularly when the American Camping Association — which is not a militant group — endorsed the Daniels proposals. Although Kurman had been around politicians enough by now to know that most of them were banal lightweights, he still had faith that change would come. At the hearing, he finished his testimony by saying: "I want to thank you, Chairman Daniels. I think it is a wonderful thing when an ordinary citizen of this country can go before the representatives that we have and get a hearing such as I have had. It certainly does far, far more for my feelings toward this wonderful country we live in than anything I have ever read in textbooks or anything else, and I want to thank you very much." Dan Krivit, who was present for these words, said that some of the politicians were touched by Kurman's sincerity. "He sounded almost corny, even a little pious. But nobody in the room moved a muscle or shuffled a paper when he spoke."

Daniels and Krivit, as disappointed as Kurman that nothing resulted from the hearings in the 90th Congress, immediately called witnesses for a new set of hearings early in the first session of the 91st Congress. By now Kurman was becoming a wise pool player, wise to all the political angles between which legislation continually caroms. He became a regular visitor to Washington, going up and down the halls of the Cannon office building, the Rayburn building, the new

Senate office building and the old Senate office building,
spreading out his facts to the politicians and their aides. He
found senators more congenial. "They are in for six years,
so they are free from the pressure the representative gets.
Their constituency is wider also, so they don't have to fear
the special-interests groups." In the House, Kurman was
often amazed to find friendly receptions from men and women
who "were on the wrong side of every issue I cared about except youth camp safety. On this, they wanted a strong law,
and they said so. I remember when I came back home and
told my wife that I talked with Gerald Ford of Michigan
and that he supported the Daniels bill. My wife thought I
was kidding." * Following hearings, the best bill to get out of
the committee was one calling for a survey. An authorization
of $175,000 was requested. This was a weak bill, much flab-
bier than the Ribicoff bill which was now making its way
through the Senate and had, in fact, been voted on the Congress before. Kurman was bitter when the House voted down
even the weak survey bill, 152–151.

As though it was decided that a poisonous pesticide should
be sprayed once and for all at this bothersome gnat from
Westport, H. R. Gross, an Iowa Republican known for his
passion for saving the taxpayers' money (though not on
defense spending), spoke up. A survey for $175,000? asked
Gross. What folly. Gross warned that if the House did not
watch out, it would soon be sending federal "wet nurses" to
look out for the kids in camp. A columnist for the Washington *Star* also checked in with his wit. "Maybe someone ought
to make another approach" rather than the survey, wrote
John McKelway. "Why not let the National Institute of
Health see if it can find a cure for homesickness?" Turning
serious, McKelway said that if it wasn't for "that small item of

---

* Representative Gerald R. Ford is a Republican who frequently lines up
with the vested or corporate interests.

$175,000" it would "probably be safe to say this piece of legislation is the most innocuous thing to have faced the 91st Congress." Kurman had become accustomed by now to the hidden opposition of the Boy Scouts and the private-camp operators but being laughed at was devastating.

Although the public argument against federal legislation for camp safety was that the states could and should do the job themselves, Kurman believed another reason existed also — money. "Let's face it," he said, "safety cost money. Spending money for things like life vests, sturdy boats, qualified personnel, well, it means you have an expense you might otherwise cut corners on. Running a camp is a business. There's nothing wrong with that. Profits aren't evil. They only become bad when you risk lives for the sake of making more money."

Instead of being depressed by the brutal defeat he had taken, Kurman became even more dogged. He kept in close contact with Dan Krivit and Dominick Daniels. Both advised Kurman that not much more could be done in the 91st Congress; let things ride. The only source of encouragement was in two pieces of legislation that were now on the books: the Coal Mine Health and Safety Act and the Occupational Health and Safety Act. Both required that standards be set and enforced by the federal government. That Congress could approve of this kind of "federal interference" that would affect industries with earnings in the tens of billions, why couldn't a camp-safety bill — involving only one industry — be passed also? Even more compelling was another fact: if the employees of the camps were now covered by a federal safety law, why not the children? Yet even this encouragement had a bleak side to it. In 1969, Congress had passed a safety-and-health law for coal miners all right, but it had been considering the law since 1951 — eighteen years and thousands of dead workers before. Camp safety had only been an issue for six years and the total number of corpses was still only in the hundreds. Have a little patience, citizen Kurman.

Going to the post for the third time, Daniels held hearings in July 1971. The same facts of tragedy and negligence came out, facts that by now were trotted out like tired dray horses. This time, the House was faced with a choice of five bills, while in the Senate the Ribicoff bill still stood. The scene was quiet until November. Kurman again came to Washington. The pressure was on because it was known that the House would soon debate the camp-safety bills as an amendment to the Higher Education Act. I spoke with Kurman and was amazed at his fullness of hope, that he still talked as if he had discovered the outrage only that morning. "I have faith in Congress," he said. "Do you know that there are a lot of representatives I've persuaded since the last session." He ran off a few names, less known to most Americans than the second-string line-ups of baseball's expansion teams. Yet they were people who had power over our lives. On November 4, the House, working well into the evening, argued camp safety, now known as Title 19 of the Higher Education Act. Kurman had allies who knew their facts and argued forcefully.

John Dent of Pennsylvania: "Does anybody in this place really believe that these camps in America are all safe and quiet little havens? Let me tell you something. The brochures they have in most instances on these camps are so antiquated that they do not even cover or resemble what the camp looks like when the children are sent there by their parents. Anybody can be hired. No one needs to pass any kind of examination or test of any kind. There is not even a simple qualification or requirement as to their ability for training or anything. A camp is an open place with absolutely no requirements as to who can run them and who cannot run them or who shall be allowed to run them. This is the only place in the whole activity of youth in the entire country where there is not one single federal regulation as to even minimum requirements for safety."

Joining Dent was Ben Rosenthal, a Queens, New York, Democrat. "As the situation stands today, nineteen states have no regulations regarding camp safety. Forty have no standards for counselors or waterfront personnel and twenty-nine states require no inspections of camp facilities. Clearly, the states have been negligent in supervising camp safety. The result of this laxity has been tragic injury and death."

Another voice was from a New York Republican, Peter Peyser. Referring to the arguments calling for inaction or delay, he said, "I must say I am a little amazed by some of the things I am hearing said about camp safety here. There is a problem of camp safety but people seem to be saying, 'We do not have any statistics dealing with safety in camps.' Statistics are very simple. I have a list right here of thirty-five children killed this past summer, and this is one section of the country. They were all killed in camps; killed in accidents, for the most part, which never should have happened. There were six drownings with no lifeguards on duty. Six were killed in a truck with a teen-age girl driving on the highway, who had no proper license to drive a group of children, and there were no regulations in the camp as to who would or could drive. We have lists from California, New Hampshire, Connecticut, Massachusetts, Minnesota, Oklahoma — I can name all these states with deaths in this year. There were thousands of accidents.

However persuasive these arguments were, Jake Pickle of Austin, Texas, would have none of it. His opposition remained firm. For one thing, "as an Eagle Scout, I think I know what safety means in any camp . . . Let us not get trapped into supporting the Daniels bill . . . Support my

substitute, and then we can have a study and have some facts
to determine what to do." Ironically Pickle was now calling
for the same survey idea which two years earlier had been
voted down by the House and mocked by the Washington
Star columnist. "This is progress," Kurman said. "We will
eventually have a camp-safety law. Everyone knows this, so
the people like Pickle try to poke along in slow motion because they know they can't stop it. I can't give up. I have to
keep snapping at them." The position of Eagle Scout Pickle
was based less on the rightness or wrongness of the issue than
on what his constituents demanded. Pickle said on the House
floor that he had numerous wires from "a dozen or more major camps in my district strongly opposing this measure [the
Daniels bill], saying that the states ought to have the right to
enforce any such standards." Coach Darrell Royal, for example, who ran Camp Champion when he wasn't on the grid-
iron, had wired Pickle. So did the Dallas YMCA "representing many of the YMCAs of Texas."* Pickle did not come on
as a Neanderthal who wanted the law of the cave to prevail.
Instead, he pictured himself as one who truly cared about the
children. "Everyone," he said, "is in favor of camp safety.
There is not a man or woman in this Chamber who would
vote against saving the lives of children. But Mr. Chairman,
we must mix in some judgment with our fervor. I think the
intent of the committee's legislation is good and I support
that intent. However, I think we may be premature in our
action today. This legislation would create a new bureaucracy with strong regulations, inspections, and enforcement
through fines and injunctions. Mr. Chairman, I will read-
ily admit and even support legislation which might save the
life of even one child away at camp. I know in my own mind
that there are camps in this country which may need policing

* David Kurman's drowning was at a YMCA camp.

. . . I do not think we know enough about the problems of camp safety. I am not certain in my own mind if the bill before us even goes to the heart of the matter. And before we jump with the solution, I think we would be wise first to survey the needs. I think we should first have a comprehensive study to seek out the basics like, how many camps exist, who runs them, what kind of safety training exists for their personnel, what is the true accident record, and all the pertinent questions which must be asked."

H. R. Gross, Mr. Money Saver, was not heard this time around on the idea of the survey, even though the cost was now up to $300,000. As a final irony, Gross joined Jake Pickle and 182 others in voting for the survey amendment of Pickle and against the standards bill of Daniels. Only 166 supported the latter. The survey amendment joined the Ribicoff bill in the Senate and went into conference committee — a parliamentary device where a final bill is drawn up in closed sessions, reconciling differences between House and Senate versions. The Ribicoff bill, while superior to the survey, was still basically weak because it only allowed states to adopt HEW standards, rather than requiring them to do so. Thus, if Texas or any state doesn't want to get in line, it doesn't have to. Indeed, there is small chance they will. Oddly, one Texas congressman who has been friendly to Kurman and who voted against the Pickle survey and for the Daniels bill, was Bob Eckhardt. "I was under a great deal of pressure to oppose the legislation [the Daniels bill] and received many letters from camp owners and directors from all over the Southwest," Eckhardt wrote Kurman. "I cannot tell you how much I admire your fine work. It is most unfortunate that it takes such personal tragedies to wake the country up. I sometimes fear, however, that the power of the special-interest lobby groups to defeat pro-people programs is limitless."

I was with Mitch and Betty Kurman in Westport in mid-
spring 1972 when the conference committee was wrangling
over the Pickle and Ribicoff bills. Kurman was in high spirit,
at the prospect that the committee would go along with the
Ribicoff approach. "I'm sure they will," he said with excitement. "They know what a long fight this has been. They
know what kind of action is needed, and even then the Ribicoff approach is a mild one. I've spoken to every man and
woman on the committee at least once, some of them two or
three times. They know me." Shortly before lunch, a phone
call came from Washington. Kurman took it, and five minutes later came back to the living room, stooped over, silent,
slumping into the sofa. "They settled on the Pickle survey
bill," he said.

He and Betty were silent for a few minutes, each with
their own feelings of sadness. But they had a rage too. "We
have a terrific system," Kurman said, echoing his lofty statement in the House hearings five years before. "But money
corrupts. Everybody thinks politicians have power but when
you talk to the politicians, they say 'What can I do? I'm only
one congressman, I'm helpless too.' You hear that from senators. Imagine, a United States senator saying he's helpless. I
remember talking to Hubert Humphrey — he told me there
are 'powerful forces' at work against the camp-safety bill. But
when I asked him specifically who these powerful forces
were, Humphrey had nothing to say. For the first time, he
was speechless. It comes down to this. For every profitable
industry you have a lobby to protect and a group of politicians
to protect the lobby. It's like the new double-protection door
locks that are selling so big to keep the thieves out. But the
lobbying-political complex keeps the thieves in so that the
public never sees them. But they steal and rob from us all
the same. They stole our son."

Most of the political defeats recorded in American life are

suffered by persons holding or seeking office and who, on election day, are rejected by the voters. But politicians are not the only ones who are struck down by political defeat. Common citizens, obscure, self-supporting, and in debt to nothing but a conscience, are rejected also. Newspapers and news shows are filled with reports on primary campaigns, delegate counts, the pointless polls and the useless speeches, so only occasionally is anyone aware that a struggle involving a lone citizen is going on. The defeat suffered by Mitch and Betty Kurman was filled with frustration, anguish, and gloom, yet personally the Kurmans were not beaten; they held or sought no office and they cared nothing about political parties. In reality, the defeat was one for the American politicial system, for the goal of participatory democracy that glowing speakers yak about to college students at graduation time. The story of Mitch Kurman suggests that the excitement of electing a new President may be the smelling salts by which public apathy will be revived but it will barely disturb the near-dead feelings of the wealthy industries supported by forceful lobbies and the Jake Pickles.

I continue to get calls and letters from Kurman, and I write to him. Mostly he sends along clippings of camping accidents — six kids killed here because of bald tires on the camp truck, two drowned there because of no life jackets, one kid sexually molested by a deranged camp counselor who was hired on the spot with no checking, two children killed when they slipped on a rocky ledge that a counselor led them on against the advice of a park ranger. Each story is tragic, and I wonder how Kurman can absorb it all. Each letter and call ends on the same note, that Kurman had recently been to see another congressman and had persudaded him about the need for a camp-safety law.

Chuck Virgin

THE BLUED, SCARRED FLESH on the chest of the child in the acute-burn ward of the Shriners' Burns Institute in Boston rose and fell with each heave of breath, and the bandage windings around her scabbed legs looked like mummy art. An arm jutted out in scarecrow stiffness, its flesh also chopped by scars. The little girl was a burn case. Her pajamas had caught fire one evening when she came too near a lick of flame from the oven in the family kitchen. The pajamas — made of cotton and bought in the children's-wear section of a city department store — ignited instantly, enshrouding the child in flames. By the time the parents suffocated the fire, while the child writhed and shrieked wildly, some 40 per cent of their daughter's body suffered second- or third-degree burns. On admission to the Burns Institute — one of two in the country, the other in Galveston — the parents were told a three-month stay would be needed, with at least six autograft skin operations in the next few years. The child may also retreat into a closet world of the emotions from which no door will ever open.

I was at the institute with Chuck Virgin, a self-employed upholsterer from Tilton, New Hampshire. I came to meet him through Frank Pollock of Consumer's Union, Pollock saying that Virgin "is a guy you should meet." Reporters hear that all the time and, for me at least, I have enough trouble getting trapped with people I shouldn't meet. Around the same time, though, two other people said the same, that Virgin would be worth meeting, that he was a man standing alone. "My son was almost burned alive," Virgin said, when I met him a few weeks later in the lobby of the Burns Institute. "It happened at five in the morning. Jimmy was up early and went downstairs by himself. He played for a little while and somehow he got his hands on a candle on the living room table. He lit it. A few seconds later, the candle tipped over on his lap. The pajamas — I bought them in a local store — went up in flames almost instantly. Jimmy couldn't react. All he could do was run upstairs and into my room. It was a scene of grief and horror. I rolled a blanket over him, smothering the flames." By mid-afternoon that February 1970 day, Jimmy Virgin was in the acute-burn ward of the institute, his life changed forever — for the worse — because someone sold his unsuspecting parents a pair of flammable pajamas. The child had 25 per cent second- and third-degree burns. He spent sixty days in the acute ward, forty-two of them in an intensive-care tent. The trunk of his body is almost entirely skin graft, extending from the lower tissue of the neck. Since the accident to his son, Chuck Virgin has traveled throughout New Hampshire telling other parents about flammable fabrics, trying to get them banned from the stores and trying to get the statehouse politicians to ban them.

That his own child was burned is tragic enough to Virgin, but another horror is even more grim: the same type pajamas that burned Jimmy are still on sale at the same store. The situation can be projected nationally. According to John Locke, chief of the Injury Study Unit at the Food and Drug Administration's Boston office and who investigates burn cases, children's sleepwear is bought every day by consumers across the country who do not suspect or realize that the garments are flammable. "It's not just the cheap imported clothing that goes up in flames," said Locke, "but also the sleepwear clothing sold in the better stores and made by the better companies. Children's clothing that burns can be

bought anywhere at any time." It is likely that only the
most alert shopper is aware of this hazard. "Time and
again," said Locke, "when I visit the parents of a child killed
or injured by burned sleepwear, they tell me how they never
dreamed their child's pajamas could catch fire so easily."
Nor did they dream that stores sell them, manufacturers
make them, and that the federal government does little to
stop either. An estimated 3000 to 5000 deaths associated
with flammable fabrics occur annually; injuries are between
150,000 to 250,000. The highest risk groups are children and
the elderly. A 1966 survey by the National Fire Protection
Association said that a large majority of those burned "were
wearing ordinary street clothing followed by nightwear."

"It's really too much to think about," Virgin said when he
showed me around the Burns Institute, where he comes with
his son almost every week for therapy. "We're burning five
thousand people a year, killing them. We know the cause, so
it's not as if we were still trying to discover a sinister germ,
like in cancer research. Yet almost nothing is done to protect
people. How can you think about this for too long? It's like
looking into the face of the sun — you'd destroy yourself.
Yet it has to be thought about. It has to be changed. The
country is filled with kids who are marked for the burn
ward."

On the desktops of federal officials, politicians, and textile
lobbyists, and far from the charred flesh of burn victims, a
debate has been going on for years as to what the federal
Flammable Fabrics Act should be doing to lower the risk of
clothing ignitions. What would seem to Chuck Virgin as a
matter of mere humane concern that disaster does not strike
another child is seen in another way by those who debate.
For them, the issue of whether the Flammable Fabrics Act is
strong or weak is a matter of compliance feasibility, consumer acceptance, and profits. Thus, although the public has

had the "protection" of flammable-fabrics legislation for eighteen years, people's clothing continues to catch fire and the government does little more than yawn. But the yawns are impressive. Congress passed the Flammable Fabrics Act in 1953 with words that would, on paper, put out the fires decisively: "any article of wearing apparel" or "fabric" so highly flammable as "to be dangerous when worn by individuals" was to be outlawed. But the law's test procedures did no more than to put off the market a few extremely hazardous items, such as the infamous brushed rayon "torch" sweaters. William White, the former executive director of the National Commission on Product Safety and later with the Federal Drug Administration's Bureau of Product Safety, said that "the test procedure of the nineteen fifty-three act is notorious for allowing ninety-nine per cent of all fabrics involved in serious burn cases to pass." One of White's staff men said that the act was so weak that in twelve years of analyzing fabrics from burn cases, only one failed. In a 1968 survey, the flammability standards were met by 117 nightgowns and garments found on the corpses of nine burn victims, and on the bodies of 74 others who were injured.

Here and there, excluding the enraged like Chuck Virgin, people looked at the Flammable Fabrics Act. Senator Warren Magnuson, who wrote the original bill and who as chairman of the Senate Commerce Committee has long battled the textile industry, has noted that "the safety issue in fabrics is that they all burn. Some burn more furiously than others. We have chemical treatments that can retard flammability, but the industry does not generally market garments made of flame-resistant fabric. It has a duty to produce garments for those persons most likely to be injured from fires — children and the elderly."

Duty? What does that mean to an industry where *ethics* is a rarely used word. The 1953 act — called dangerously permissive by White — was amended in 1967, with the Commerce Department given power to set new standards for clothing and other household fabrics. In contrast to their support of the weak 1953 act, the textile industry, fearing a dark cloud might be set loose into their sunny skies of profit, balked and moaned about the new powers proposed for the Commerce Department. Howard A. Heffron, a Washington attorney, in his June 1970 report to the Commission on Product Safety said that the industry "railed against the 1967 amendments." The statements of fabric makers, he said, varied from the naive and ingenious to the cynical and callous." He quoted a spokesman for the National Retail Merchants Association before a House hearing: "It is an unfortunate condition of life that a certain number of individuals in every age group will die in any selected interval of time and that whatever the forces that determine the random distribution of death, they will result in some number of deaths attributable to fire.

". . . A single untimely death and a single burn is one too many, but how far should legislative regulation be carried in attempts to reduce death and suffering caused by flammable apparel when such regulation will reduce for the total population its capacity for living a life of free choice."

One man who has loathing contempt for the industry thinking is Dr. John Constable, a plastic surgeon at the Burns Institute and on the Harvard Medical School faculty; he treats many of the victims of the textile industry's violence, including Jimmy Virgin. "It's long been known that children's nightwear — in fact, all of a child's clothes or those of a person of any age — can be made flame-resistant. The textile industry could do it any time it wants. After all, the draperies and curtains in nightclubs are made flame-resistant. That's required by the government. But for the kids, nothing. It's economics, only economics. Pajamas or T-shirts made, for example, from flame-resistant material that costs a dollar or two a yard more will not be priced much higher than untreated garments. But the manufacturers are afraid of competitors and consumer reaction. Unless the textile people know that every garment of the same type would have to be flame-resistant, they will not market them. They're afraid of losing money."

The power of the 1967 amendments was in its potential — finally, the government could move in with strong restrictive standards, perhaps like the one in Britain where, since 1967, all children's sleepwear must be flame-retardant and all adult sleepwear be labeled if it does not pass the tests. But in three and a half years, the government's powerful muscle had hardly been flexed. Only one new standard was set — for rugs — and no standard for clothing. The Secretary of Commerce was given the power to call an advisory committee meeting to discuss proposals, but nearly one and a half years passed before such a meeting was called. Pressure from public criticism, the burn statistics gathered by the FDA, and hearings of the Commerce Committee gathered with such force that the department finally agreed to propose a standard for children's sleepwear. This was in November of 1970; then-Secretary Maurice H. Stans called it "tough but realistic."

In matters of regulation, it is often government policy to set a proposed standard and then wait for public comment on it. Middle-level officials who write the standards speak of this "public comment" aspect as if the citizens awake every morning to shoot off letters to the government on the latest proposal. Actually, the average citizen knows little or nothing of this process. Occasionally public officials will tell of the mail they receive on a particular issue — a favorite device of Richard Nixon's, as in October 1971 when he read letters from the common man on his economic freeze — but this

mail gets only a form letter in return. Those who watch the
proposed safety-and-health standards closest are the lobbies
and industries themselves.

Thus, when Stans proposed a ban on children's sleepwear
up to the size of 6X — meaning for children five and under
— there was no outpouring of consumer opinion while the
response from the textile industry was heavy. George S.
Buck, Jr., director of research at the National Cotton Council
in Memphis, used words ironically familiar in burn wards to
express his views on the proposed standard: "a nightwear
nightmare." In the form it now takes, said Buck, "it appears to me that the standard is one small step toward safety
and one giant leap toward confusion and chaos." Among the
effects of the standard, if it is to be passed, Buck said that
"mothers will be unable to purchase for their children any
lightweight, cool, absorbent nightwear for hot-weather use.
All children's nightwear will cost substantially more — conservatively from 25 to 50 per cent. Many nightwear items
will have reduced service life — perhaps one half to one
third of the present wear life . . . Textile mills and finish-
ers processing thousands of yards of cloth per hour will be required to use quality control tests which, at best, take several
days to perform."

Industry spokesmen who made sure their lobbying was
felt included Fred Fortress of the Celanese Fibers Marketing Company. He asked for "reasonable" standards. His
arguments, similar to ones heard from the auto industry concerning antipollution devices, included: technology is not
yet practical, demands for action come from people who have
little understanding of the problem, and not enough is known
about the circumstances that lead to ignition.

To understand why Howard Heffron's statement that the
textile industry is "cynical and callous" is accurate, it must
be remembered that the industry's giant protest about the

proposed standard centered on less than 1 per cent of textile production.

In July 1971, when the standard came out as law, Commerce Department officials praised themselves for their "boldness." In taking on less than 1 per cent of the industry's production quota, the result is that the burning continues. "The new standard is a step forward, but far short of what it should be," said John Locke, the FDA man in Boston who sees in the flesh the results of flammable fabrics. "Three high-risk groups are still not protected: children under six not wearing sleepwear — but perhaps dresses or playclothes to bed — or are wearing sleepwear larger than six X, which is common. Then there are the children between ages six and fourteen, one of the largest groups where children get burned. And third, the elderly: they are ten per cent of the population but twenty per cent of the burned-clothing cases. All in all, if this new standard had been in effect for the last three years, only ten per cent of the clothing ignitions seen by our office would have been protected."

No proposals are being made by the government for protecting the tens of thousands of citizens who are daily in danger of burns from flammable clothing. Senator Magnuson, an ally of consumers, says that no single bill he has worked on has been "so bitter a disappointment" as the Flammable Fabrics Act. He makes charges that the Commerce Department is unwilling and unable to protect the unsuspecting public from fire-trap clothing, but his voice means little. Even when he says the fabrics program should be taken away from the Commerce Department; this is only talk, which the industry and its powerful lobby knows.

A debate, a small one, goes on about how soon a new standard will be proposed. Meanwhile, there are still the scenes of horror in the burn wards. The parents of those children had assumed that the government and the textile industry were protecting their young ones. "But we were wrong," said Chuck Virgin, "and now we have our whole lives to think about it. The trouble comes when children act like children — occasionally going near candles, ovens, and heaters or innocently fooling with matches or lighters. A lick of flame may ignite their clothing and cause serious burns. Technology is available to reduce these injuries but the people in power leisurely debate the issue as though they were deciding a change in the rules of gin rummy. That they are so detached is almost as shocking as the sight of a burned child."

Virgin has become what the rest of us, in our uneasiness with people who get worked up, call "a crusader." Since the accident to his boy, he has been traveling up and down New Hampshire alerting other parents. The state is full of town meeting halls and houses, so he hits them regularly. The Lions, Elks, Knights of Columbus, and the rest also have their places, and Virgin has told the story of flammable fabrics dozens, even hundreds, of times there. His goal, one he realizes is mythic, is to defeat the textile industry, to get it to manufacture clothes and garments that do not burn. "You'd think I was asking for them to stop the machines in the mills. I've run into textile people and they act as if I'm out to destroy them. Naturally, they call me a Communist. I'm destructive. And they're right. I'm destructive to fires. I have this strange hang-up — wanting to put them out. Especially, when kids are catching fire."

Richard D'Ambrosio

WHAT CAN YOU SAY about a twelve-year-old girl, hideously deformed, withdrawn in eerie muteness, diagnosed as schizophrenic, the unwanted child of alcoholic parents, stashed away in a public hospital at eighteen months? Not much can be said. Basket cases never draw wordy comments from society. America has too many solvable problems to worry about without taking on the sure losers. The name of the girl is Laura. The love involved in her story is the kind seldom seen in a culture where forces try to con us into believing that love is just a matter of "connecting," and has nothing to do with sacrifice, patience, or sorrow. The man who loved this child was a practicing psychoanalyst in Brooklyn, Dr. Richard D'Ambrosio. I know him only through the book he wrote, *No Language but a Cry*. Except for an excellent review in *Commonweal* and excerpts here and there, the book, published in the summer of 1970, received little attention. At the time, much of the reading public was taken with a novel called *Love Story*, a worthless clutter of fictional nonsense, and so had no taste for a true love story that demanded commitment and strain. I include the story of Richard D'Ambrosio and Laura because their love story is an example of nonadjustment in its most solitary form: a one-to-one relationship. The peace that the psychiatrist disturbed was only his own, the peace and comfort of a psychiatric practice that had plenty of challenges without the near impossible one of reaching into the deep silences of a battered child.

Laura first came to the attention of the world at eighteen

months in Brooklyn. Throughout her infancy, her mother
and father, one drinker unhappily paired to another drinker,
regularly beat the child during alcoholic rages. They
mauled her with fists and straps, causing welts the size of rai-
sins. The child's only protests from her crib were shrieks and
moans. This only enraged her parents more. One night
neighbors noticed the crying had more animality to its wail
than before. They called a policeman. He crashed into the
apartment and, led by the sound of the shrieks, went to the
kitchen. There, in a large frying pan over a high flame, amid
a black-brown smoke and the sound of sizzling, Laura was
being burned alive by her parents.

This night of misery passed. Hospital doctors, rising to
the rare medical challenge of reviving cooked flesh, brought
the infant's body back to life. Laura's mind was something
else. In the following months, she rarely moved, ate poorly,
avoided play objects, and sat for hours on the hospital floor
in a blank trance, an escapee of hell deported to limbo. At
age three, still hospitalized, her eyes were crossed, her spine
had a severe curvature, and the veins of her legs were vari-
cosed. By five, Laura had yet to pronounce a word. She could
not walk without help. Tests showed an IQ of 50. Some doctors, weary of hopeless child-abuse cases, labeled her men-
tally deficient, while others saw her ghastly withdrawal as
schizophrenia.

Plans were made to dump the child in a state mental hospital. These inns of despair were filled, though. By chance,
a group of Catholic sisters belonging to an order devoted
to child care had room for Laura. The public has seen much
of Catholic sisters the past few years, with the FBI (full of
Catholics, ironically) tapping their minds and judges jail-
ing them for keeping silent about their pacifism. But the
best of the nuns — meaning nearly all of them — are still devoted to the thankless works of mercy and rescue that every

society needs, especially this one. Laura's sisters rose at 5
A.M., retired at midnight, seven days a week. The city
government gave them some money, the rest they obtained
by begging.

The sisters did everything for Laura. They had to. During
her seven years at the home — and the sisters made it a true
home — the child never spoke a word. She didn't play or
smile. She remained a lone citizen in her world of withdrawn numbness. Many Catholic sisters, when you get to
know them, say the hardest thing for them is to keep alive
belief in God; spiritual aridity dries up any feeling of a personal diety. Yet, in many ways, belief in God is often very
easy when compared to believing in a human being like
Laura, to whom life is so painfully absent. Heroically, the
sisters refused to despair, living out Cardinal Newman's remark about faith in God: "A thousand difficulties do not
make one doubt." In embracing the ugly and deformed
child, they made one of the harder acts of faith become one of
the harder acts of love.

A young psychiatrist visited the home by chance one day.
At first, he said little could be done for Laura. The sheer
atrocity of her frying-pan trauma had forever pushed the
child behind a protective wall of fantasy. But the doctor,
given a choice of a hundred other kids, asked to work with
Laura. Session after session, first weeks, months, then years,
the psychiatrist tried for two-way communication. It remained one-way, from him to her. His friendship and work
received nothing in return but mute stares. Only a rare
tear down Laura's cheek gave evidence that within her hunch-
backed body an emotional life existed.

After hundreds of hours of social and play therapy, a mo-
mentous breakthrough came: the child accepted a candy bar
one day from the psychiatrist. Normal children learn the
mechanism — grasping a desirable object — at two or three

months. Elated at this progress, and in spite of the quick emotional retreat following it, the doctor invested more and more of his own time and practice. Another breakthrough came. While the two walked on a street near the home one afternoon, a group of raucous boys on roller skates came blustering by. Laura grabbed at the doctor's waist for protection. Like anyone else, she reacted to fear by reaching out to another person. Laura was not psychotic after all, thought the psychiatrist, who felt like singing.

Finally, his patient turtled back into her shell of silence, the psychiatrist built a miniature house where a toy family lived. He moved them around, staging a fight between the parents that ended in a beating for the baby. "No, no, no," screamed Laura, rising in contortion from the chair. Her body quivered with fifteen years of suppressed rage at this reenacted scene from her infancy. For the doctor, the screaming was the greatest single sound he had ever heard.

No false hopes were built up by the psychiatrist that Laura would ever be normal, but a long-shot chance existed nevertheless. Operations were planned to improve her eyes, back, legs, and facial scars. Meanwhile, her silent rage released, Laura's speech improved almost by itself. In time, she went to classes at a nearby school. With great catch-up skills, she soon became much like the other teen-agers in the home. Like boomerangs returning to past squalor, Laura's parents — now out of the mental hospital — came around. The child rejected them both.

Laura left the home and care of Dr. D'Ambrosio at age eighteen, a high school graduate, her body recovered, and her mind repaired. She received vocational training and soon found a job — as a pediatrics nurse.

PART IV

Farmers with a View

The Tri-Township Citizens Association

MOST OF THE JOURNALISTS I know, men and women who work in cities and who brave daily the speed and crowdedness of urban ways, have strong affections for farms. For some, this attraction of the heart is easily figured, coming in the form of regular withdrawals from one's storehouse of dreams — "someday I'm going to settle down and buy myself a little farm," they say. Others are soft because a farm experience is less a dream of the future than a memory of the past. One morning, when the editorial writers of the Washington *Post* were holding our daily meeting, the subject of farming came up, a momentary diversion from the regular run of mischief calling for comment. Nearly everyone there, eight writers, had a farm story to tell, based on personal experience. One worked in a henhouse in his boyhood, another herded goats, another had tended cattle one summer in Wyoming. En route to their adulthoods in the city, these stopovers on the farms now held honored places in their memories. In the newsroom of the *Post,* a reporter, talking about his year on a farm, told me, "That's one stretch in my life when everything made sense."

My own stretch was five and a half years. The Trappists were traditionally bound to the land through the sixth century Rule of St. Benedict and its practical urgings for the fathers and brothers to grow their own food for their own table. The community in Georgia had some 400 acres, about a third under cultivation. When I went there in August 1960, the brother in charge of assigning work — called the cellarer, from the old days of the wine cellar — examined what he called the fancy cut of my clothes, flowered slacks, a yellow shirt, and white shoes. "You look fit for the manure pile," he said. Apparently, he thought the work would be too much for me: scraping clean the dairy-barn floor after 100 cows were milked, shoveling the manure into wheelbarrows, dumping it behind the barn and then loading it all — a few hundred pounds by now — onto a manure spreader. It would be deposited back in the corn and sorghum fields, starting again the natural rhythm: the manure fertilized the fodder, the cows ate the fodder, the food was digested, and part of it became manure and was returned to the fields. But I liked the work fine, considering myself a student of one of nature's oldest crash courses. After six months of manure, and seeing I had been "tested," the cellarer promoted me to the milking crew. For the next four years, excepting one day when I stayed in bed relaxing a back strained from lifting a paralyzed heifer, I milked Jerseys twice a day, 2 A.M. and 2 P.M. Both shifts took four hours. The bold idea of doing this for the rest of my life never took hold, but doing it for a few years seemed exactly right, an invitation to the green world of farming that, once left, I would probably never get back to.

Never has not entirely been the case. What this country is doing to the small farmer — such things as squeezing him off the land for housing developments, forcing him to use chemicals or else be unable to compete with agri-business prices — is an ongoing news story, one that I try to cover, if only on occasion and from a distance. Among the farms I have visited — in Virginia, Maryland, Pennsylvania, and Florida — all were run by men not only committed to the land but committed to a philosophy that refused adjustment to commercialization. It is a strange turn. One hundred years ago, surviving on the land meant successfully battling the ferocities of weather, isolation, wildlife, in short, the unknown. Today, many small farmers battle enemies that are known only too well: the powerful trade associations that lobby for pro agri-business laws at the expense of the small operator, the lazy federal agencies — the Agriculture Department, the Food and Drug Administration — that protect the vested interests rather than the public's interest. That the small farmer can be passed off so easily is not a new disgrace, nor even a new attitude. Sean O'Casey condemned it in the last essay he wrote, "The Bald Primaqueera," published in the *Atlantic Monthly* in 1965. "The strangest thing of all is the foolish and hateful way in which playwrights and critics regard the farm workers as ignorant, stupid, and given to ferocity. It is an odd contemplation of the country worker, and could be very questionable if it were not ridiculous. Even in my early days, although the field workers were often ignorant in the ways of formal education, they were never stupid, were highly intelligent as far as the farming knowledge of the time went, and had a great deal of natural knowledge. They had none of the gaudy or gorgeous knowledge of the higher airs within them, but they were well versed in the knowledge of the good earth they husbanded, of the earth that gave us life and provides the wherewithal to maintain it. They knew the odd ways of the sky, the clouds, the wind and the rain, the ways of the Farmer's Boy, and all the ways of the things around them, the fields, the animals, wild and domestic, the trees, the silent turmoil that went on in hedge and pond, and all this made them one with most remarkable mysteries of life."

The mysteries of life in Liberty Township, Adams County, Pennsylvania, were the ancient and simple ones based on the truth that nature is an ally, not a foe. Liberty Township's people are quiet and individualistic. Although the vacuum of progress is slowly sucking in the farm business of many of the citizens, they are determined not to be pulled away without a struggle. In January 1970, the Tri-Township Citizens Association was formed, with an original membership of forty-two. I happened to be visiting the area late in the summer of that year — a day in the country, up from Washington about seventy miles. Looking at the wide sweep of the beautiful land, rich in wildlife, you would think it the last place to be touched by the grabby fingers of politicians and corporationists. But they are there, trying to take more and more from farmers who have less and less.

Ray Sowers is one of those farmers. He had been having trouble with his pond for a few years, seeing it change from a clear-water basin where his cattle could water to a polluted sink hole where they would get sick. Sowers lived simply, but not so simply that he didn't have hunches on why his once clean pond was suddenly mucky and undrinkable: soil erosion. In October 1970, he filed a complaint with the U.S. Soil Conservation office in nearby Gettysburg against Charnita, Inc., a land-development company that had been selling, and still sells, retirement and vacation homesites in Adams County. Charnita is a publicly held firm that owns 2500 acres in Adams County, with reported options to buy more. By 1968, Charnita sales totaled $6 million; by May 1970, 2900 lots had been sold, many to Washington-area residents. The invasion of Charnita made life tense and painful for Sowers and the others in the Citizens Association. His struggles to survive and his refusals to adjust went far beyond the fences of his 125-acre farm. They penetrated the complex politics of ecology, suggesting that this society is only faintly aware of the hard and costly choices still to be made if nature is to stay balanced.

After Sowers' complaint, the conservation men from Gettysburg came out to look around his farm and the neighboring land of Charnita. When I visited the officials at their office, they confirmed that Sowers' pond was indeed polluted by soil from Charnita erosion. The official was a native of the area who had no mind to take on powerful Charnita, but neither was he the good bureaucrat who looked the other way. "There's been little or nothing done by Charnita about soil-erosion control. We'd have cooperated with them on this problem but they never asked us. The new Charnita ski slope has land fill that erodes when it rains, and of course the sediment winds up in Sowers' pond. With minimum concern, Charnita could take care of this. Even thirty minutes of work with a bulldozer would have corrected Mr. Sowers' problem, diverting the water away. But Charnita never even did this. They knew we could have helped him — free of cost."

Near the pond on the Sowers' farm is the henhouse. A large-sized flock of Rhode Island Reds are housed there, good layers that provide Sowers with a modest income. But problems began in the summer of 1970 when Charnita built an airport near Sowers' farm. The flight patterns were such that planes zoomed out and swooped in over his henhouses. The noise scares the sensitive birds silly; indeed, the afternoon I walked through the henhouse, the birds were in what Sowers kindly called "a state." Hens need an environment of calmness to do their laying, or at least to do it with any regularity.* Sowers said he had nothing against airplanes, but coming in low over his birds meant, in the end, a lowered income for him. He complained to a state aviation official,

* I learned this not from a book, but firsthand at the Trappist farm in Georgia. Twenty thousand hens were there in three sprawling houses. The brother in charge told me one day — in sign language — that his birds were so sensitive that whenever there was a thunderstorm in the night, some seven days later egg production dropped. He showed me a chart he kept — with occasional dips. A thunderstorm was responsible, he said. The birds, frightened by the strange noises, suffered a disturbance of their psyches which affected the lead time in the internal development of the eggs. If any stage of the process is bothered, it will show up later.

asking for relief. Nothing happened on the complaint, Sowers
said, so I volunteered to call the official. Unlike the soil-erosion man, the aviation official was glad to see Charnita in
Adams. He said it was progress. "The airport is legal and
certified," he said. "The people in Liberty should be
real proud of it. It means they're going forward." The official acknowledged that Sowers was not consulted before the
license permit was issued. I asked him about Sowers' henhouses and his claim of decreased egg production. He
laughed at that one. "We have lots of airports with flight
patterns that go over chickens. At first, they think it's a loud
hawk up there. Then the chickens get used to it."

The Citizens Association that Sowers joined was at first little more than a group of commiserators. Corporations have
never much worried about these groups; the latter gets mad,
joins together, signs a petition, and then, when things stay
the same, breaks up in despair. The organized system beats
the unorganized citizens. Some members of the association,
though, had the sense to begin their struggle armed with legal documents, not scatter-shot anger. An early clue to
Charnita's land-development practices was found; the farmers noticed that Charnita's sales program included lots in
swampy meadowland, sites the natives well knew would be
unsuitable for the construction of many houses with septic
tanks. The soil could never absorb the sewage. The farmers
knew this and so did Charnita, but the buyers wouldn't.
Members of the association rummaged through the usually
ignored township files at the county courthouse and discovered a document called the "Sewage Facilities Plan for
Liberty Township" prepared in August 1969 by township
engineers. The report summarized that "it is best to assume
the soil conditions to be 'severe' or 'hazardous' in the areas
presently under development and a public or community
sewage collection system should be installed as soon as possi-

ble. Consideration should also be given to the installation of a municipal water system because of the definite possibility of groundwater contamination." Discovering this needle of fact in the haystack of bureaucracy was a rare find, and the group made immediate use of it. Dr. Dagmar Perman, a Washington historical writer who with her husband owned forty acres of land adjacent to Charnita, made a legal complaint to the Department of Housing and Urban Development. With help from ecology-minded lawyers, including one from the American Civil Liberties Union, HUD was prodded into action. Dr. Perman's complaint led HUD to order Charnita to put on the cover of its property report — a document all potential buyers of lots must be shown before signing the contract — a caution that "many areas of land in this development may not be suitable for on-site sewage disposal [septic tanks] . . ."

At first, the HUD decision showed the farmers that they had power and that perhaps the government might be an ally after all. Ten months after the HUD decision, though, the tough wording on Charnita's caution was replaced by substitute language referring the reader to fine-print paragraphs within the report. The farmers, sniffing a sellout, wondered about the change; it seemed odd since the soil hadn't changed. Through a few phone calls in Washington, I learned that the substitute language was requested by the Pennsylvania attorney general's office on two occasions. HUD had granted both requests.

One of Sowers' fellow farmers in Liberty was Bill Brent, an apple grower who often won the "best bushel award" at state fairs and who was the chairman of the Citizens Association. He was dismayed at the HUD shift. "They backed off," he said. "Their original decision was certainly not made lightly. It was based on legal and conclusive evidence. It seems strange that the federal government in an interstate dispute would yield to a state official. Here in Adams County, once a farmer says he'll do something, he does it. His word means something." A HUD official disputed Brent's charge, as naturally he would. "We have not backed off our enforcement program with Charnita. We are continuing to cooperate with Pennsylvania state officials. Charnita has done what we asked them to do." "That's exactly right," said Mrs. Perman. "Charnita did what HUD asked. It's just that they didn't keep at it."

If the politicians and bureaucrats at federal and state levels caved in, the local counterparts matched them. Fearing possible pollution of the local creeks that meander through their farmlands, the association made a legal complaint to the State Health Department. Charnita had a sewage-treatment plant for its recreation facilities but nothing was planned for sewage from lots and homesites other than septic tanks. In June 1970, an order came from the health office forbidding housing construction on all Charnita lots until a central sewerage system could be planned. Two months later, however, the health office partially lifted the ban, allowing building on a small number of lots pending construction of a central sewerage system. One reason for this change was the decision of the three-member Liberty Township board of supervisors to make Charnita's sewer problems a municipal responsibility. In other words, the people would bear the major part of the cost, not the corporation. The one board member who believed Charnita should finance its own sewerage system was John Flenner, an Adams County farm worker. "I opposed this and was astounded when the other two board members approved. Charnita was originally required legally — by the land-subdivision resolutions — to pay for the cost of all their sewers and other improvements. Now suddenly it is we and the unsuspecting lot owners in Charnita who will be paying for the sewers."

With the possibility of having to help pay for the sewer system, the local farmers were now caught in an even tighter economic squeeze. Over the last few years, the development's presence had automatically raised the assessment value of local land. According to Bill Brent, from 1965 to 1970, the real-estate tax doubled. This is bad enough, but from the small farmer's view it is even worse: the yield of the land remained the same, the harvested produce, the lumber hauls. Because Charnita's presence had "enriched" the area, the state was passing on less and less money for the community's needs. "I'm trapped, that's all," said Olmer Spence, a farmer in the association.

The citizens' group did win a small and unexpected victory in the spring of 1972. HUD, which had shuffled its personnel around in a try for a new hand, took action against Charnita by forbidding it to make any future sales of lots. However decisive this HUD action appeared, Bill Brent and Dagmar Perman were not elated. "HUD has swung the big stick before," said Dr. Perman, "but then backed away when the pitches came in hard and fast. Maybe they mean it this time. They have new people working in the agency. But the trouble is they don't have anyone new working at Charnita. Only the old ones. And what can you do with them?"

Part of the attitude of the Charnita Corporation to the situation of farmers like Ray Sowers, Bill Brent, and the others was shown at a town meeting in Liberty. Charles G. Rist, the founder, chairman, and president of the development, in a discussion of the need for a sewer system said: "We own sixty-five per cent of the township, pay over ninety per cent of the real-estate taxes and are all registered voters here. If you don't like Charnita, then leave." In an interview with the Washington *Post*, Rist was even bolder: "I'm being harassed by half a dozen nuts." Perhaps so, but the farmers are nutty about exactly the right values: pure land, clean water, and quiet countryside. During the time the Citizens Association was tangling with Charnita, the corporation was the object of a HUD order, a Justice Department suit (settled by consent decree), and a Federal Trade Commission complaint. Few of the farmers in the association dreamed they would ever spin this complex a legal and political web when they first challenged their big neighbor. As I write now, it is still not clear how the dispute will eventually be settled. But it is not a quarrel isolated to this rural Pennsylvania town; instead, it is a part of a nationwide pattern that is pitting citizens against land developers. The Nixon Administration proposed a land-use program, but it has gone nowhere, suggesting that until government at all levels is willing to give full backing to saving the land and the people on it, the new programs will not do much except create the illusion that things are under control. Meanwhile, Ray Sowers is complaining about his dirty pond and he doesn't think his hens will ever be persuaded that those planes overhead are loud hawks.

Sam Schmidt

FOR THE PAST FEW YEARS, I have gone with my family to Vero Beach, Florida. It is still one of the undiscovered towns of Florida, although its virginity will not be lasting long; the ever-prowling American rapist, the land developer, is already coming around, eager to deflower pretty Vero with townhouses, ranch houses, beach houses, everything, it appears, but outhouses. For years, the treasured assets of this hideaway community of 10,000 were its lack of glitter — go to Palm Beach, seventy miles downcoast for that — and its slowness of step in Florida's fast march to progress — go to Orlando, 100 miles north and inland, for that. My mother and aunt have lived in Vero Beach for some years, and the three or four weeks of vacation we spend with them have been times of high feeling.

Even in Vero Beach, though, the peace is being disturbed by Sam Schmidt. He is sixty-two, a first-generation German, short with a round, bald head, slow in speech, as though he is giving out instructions. The gamble in his life came when he suffered a near-fatal heart attack in 1966. At the time, he was living in Detroit, a wealthy engineer who had risen through the ranks of the Ford Motor Company. As a boy, he had been yanked from his native Germany amid the upheavals of pre-World War I days. His mother and he came to Dearborn. Eager to be absorbed by a country full of new opportunities, at age twelve Schmidt made a tractor out of Model-T junk parts and rode it in the streets of Detroit. Henry Ford heard of this creative brashness and sent a chauffeured limousine to fetch the youngster from elementary school. The man and the boy became friends, and Schmidt went on to receive a technical education at the Henry Ford Trade School.

Following his heart attack at fifty-seven, Schmidt came to Florida to invest his money into the full-time raising of pure organic beef. He had been dabbling in cattle over the years, as a hobby where he never had to leave the office and climb over the pasture fence. After two years in Florida, Schmidt decided that he could supply safer and healthier meat than what the supermarkets were selling. He opened a meat shop — called Beefeaters Salon — in Vero Beach and went behind the counter himself to become the head butcher. On my last visit to Vero Beach, the store was doing well; customers came in all day, phone orders were being taken, and large $500 orders from out-of-state buyers were common.

Schmidt's story would end there — another small businessman keeping afloat in a sea made rough by the mighty ships of Safeway, Giant, A & P, Krogers and the others. But Sam Schmidt the butcher has a national significance when both his organically raised Kobe cattle and his philosophy of farming are compared with those dominating the American beef industry. The big companies that supply much of America's meat — Swift, Armour, Wilson — have little to fear from the competition of Beefeaters Salon in Vero Beach, yet a Miami *Herald* news story said that Schmidt's operation "may mark the beginning of a revolution in raising beef." Schmidt is a lucky businessman, because his own interest matches the public interest; it is rare that the two meet on the same track. His ultimate goal, aside from regaining his investment, "is to enable people to eat meat that is both free of added chemicals or antibiotics, and to provide meat that is low in fat. I'd be foolish to come out of a comfortable retirement just to run another butcher shop. I'm trying to do something beyond that — prove that the consumer badly wants and needs natural meat that can help his health, not block it."

The first indication that Schmidt has not adjusted to the ways of the meat industry is in the taste of his beef. It is flavorful, tender, juicy, and easily bitten into. It has none of the leathery texture or tastelessness of the steaks sold by supermarkets, or the slabs of concrete the restaurants serve up under the name of tender sirloin. An early clue that Schmidt's meat is different is in the operation of his cattle ranch at Loxahatchee, ninety miles southwest of Vero Beach. Some 1200 beef cattle graze on 2800 acres of pasture. Seven to fifteen types of grasses and grains are utilized in a unique pasture-rotation program. Cattle need variety in their diet, the same as humans do, so Schmidt's operation is designed to avoid giving the beasts the same old meal every day. Kobe cattle, black and hefty animals, are usually Aberdeen Angus bred and raised by the methods used in Kobe, Japan. Schmidt imports the Kobes from Japan by artificial insemination, impregnating the Angus mothers. Because the cattle at Loxahatchee are fed only grasses, they are given no tenderizers, no fatteners, no drugs, no preservatives, no colorings, and no harmful chemicals. In short, they get nothing artificial and the result is that the meat has little waste and little fat.

Seeing the Kobe cattle roam the wide, flat pastures of Florida seems only natural, but the uniqueness cannot be appreciated unless a typical cattle lot is seen. There, the animals are crowded in shank to shank, closely confined with thousands of others and barely allowed to walk, let alone wander about. The Kobes at Loxahatchee average one acre of pasture to feed on, as compared with the usual feedlot, where the cattle eat from a conveyor belt. Overall, the average Schmidt steer is on the pasture about three years before slaughtering, having been fattened on naturally grown food. According to the Department of Agriculture's Research Center at Beltsville, Maryland, most commercial feedlots can speed up the fattening process — by overfeeding and drug stimulation — so that a steer can be slaughtered for market at twelve to eighteen months. The overfeeding is often a malicious deed in itself; so much food is forced into the animals — by mixing the water with the feed, so the animals can quench their thirst only by eating more grain — that it would be the equivalent of a human being sitting down for a Christmas dinner three times a day every day of the year.

"Naturally, these animals get fat in a hurry," says Schmidt. "Wouldn't you get fat if you ate so much and weren't allowed to exercise? I often wonder why the humane society for animals doesn't get after the feedlot operators, instead of just worrying about stray dogs and cats stuck up in tree branches." While Schmidt prefers not to get worked up about the ethics of his fellow cattlemen — "my doctor says to stay calm and not get excited about outrages" — he insists that "you can't hurry up nature, nor can you try to trick her. A body — animal or human — cannot be tampered with for commercial reasons without risking harmful results. You cut costs all right, there's not as much bother, and sales are increased, but what are you doing to the meat and what are you doing to your health when you eat it?"

Schmidt's philosophy is assuredly not widely shared among U.S. cattlemen but it is anything but wild thinking. In a report by a Ralph Nader study group, *Sowing the Wind, the Report on Food Pesticides and the Poor as Affected by the Department of Agriculture,* the author, Harrison Wellford, writes: "With the possible exception of a few stores specializing in organically grown beef, it is virtually impossible to buy meat which is not contaminated to some degree with synthetic residues. Between 80 and 90 per cent of all beef and poultry produced in this country is grown on a diet of antibiotics and other drugs from birth to slaughter. Three fourths of all cattle in the United States are fed stilbestrol and other growth-stimulating hormones. Pesticides enter the human food chain when animals eat contaminated feed and water or are directly sprayed to control parasites and insects." The facts that Wellford mentions are not widely known, possibly because the public has enough to worry about with the higher and higher prices of meat. It has also gradually adjusted to the tastelessness of it, so few imagine there is anything else besides leathery and vapid meat. "When the public gets outraged enough at what's being done to it," Schmidt believes, "there is action. But it takes plenty to get people moving. It wasn't until I suffered a painful heart attack myself in 1966 that I really got mad enough to do something. Doctors told me I could have avoided a heart attack if I had been more careful about my diet. That's when I decided to raise beef organically in earnest. I had been doing it as a hobby for years. But it became a matter of life and death. Since then, I guess about fifty thousand people have eaten close to a million of my organic steaks, myself heading the list. Can we all be wrong?"

A second difference in Schmidt's methods of cattle raising is the absence of stilbestrol (DES, from Diethylstilbestrol) in the Kobes' diet. DES is the controversial hormone that is mixed with feed to increase the growth rate of cattle. A 1965 Florida Department of Agriculture report states that with DES, cattle can gain 18 per cent in weight on 12 per cent less feed. DES has been a profitable gimmick for the meat industry, but it has a minor drawback in that it causes cancer in lab animals.

You wonder about the ethics of an industry that would use a cancer-causing substance that has appeared in a significant number of cattle, in their livers and kidneys. Even more reason to wonder, there is the Food and Drug Administration that has yawned for years while DES was being used, and only

after Congressional pressure moved to require that cattlemen withhold DES from livestock feed seven days before
slaughter. Senator William Proxmire and Representative
Ogden Reid introduced legislation in 1972 that would ban
DES from use in cattle feed entirely, the way it is now banned
in chicken feed. Twenty-one foreign nations ban DES from
cattle feed. Much of this is too technical to arouse the interests of the meat-eating public. In *Consumer Beware,* a valuable book for survival in the shopping aisles, Beatrice Trum
Hunter tells what DES means from the customer's point of
view: DES "yields poorer meat because it produces weight
that is watery fat but not protein. It creates more marbling
of fat throughout the edible portions of the meat. This is not
only undesirable but an economic fraud. However, the problem is far graver than merely one of adulteration and low
quality. DES has been acknowledged by scientists as a potent
carcinogen, and has been labeled 'biological dynamite.' "

Because his Kobes are raised organically and at nature's
pace, not the chemists', Schmidt's greatest pride is the low fat
content of his beef. As an active member of the American
Heart Association, and a past officer of the local Indian River
County Heart Association, Schmidt sees his butcher shop as
also a health aid to the consumer. "Heart disease is a major
killer in this country. Much of this is from the meat we let
ourselves eat. Most of us think we should just avoid whipped
cream, buttered potatoes, ice cream, eggs, and things like
that. But meat — the way we allow it to be raised com-
mercially — can contribute to the cause of heart attacks
also."

To date, Schmidt has no conclusive proof that his lean meat
helps prevent heart trouble. He cites a number of local doctors who advise their cardiac patients to eat his Kobe meat.
The Miami *Herald* reported in early 1972 that a Vero
Beach veterinarian conducted a controlled test of 100 head

of cattle, half of them Kobe calves, half not. The vet found a significant lowering of cholesterol in the blood of the Kobes than in the cattle fed and raised under regular conditions.

The reason for the tenderness of Kobes is that the animals are massaged before slaughtering. "This is an integral part of the process," says Schmidt, mentioning that the average U.S. steer is never even touched, let alone massaged, during its lifetime. "Cattle get tense, especially near the end. Instead of giving them the usual tranquilizer, the Kobe method calls for the relaxing of tensions and muscle meat by massage. It's an art with the Japanese and it results in tender meat. I've tried it here and it works, though it shakes up the farm hands a bit. They're used to treating the cattle like animals."

For the layman who comes into the shop and knows little about the differences in meat except by cost, Schmidt devised a counter display that provides graphic evidence that his meat is low in fat. Attached to a display board are five four-ounce samples of cooked ground steak. One is Schmidt's, the others are from local supermarkets. Under each sample is a test tube holding all the juices and fats drained from each steak section. The Kobe beef sample had one-fourth ounce of solidified fats in the drainage total. The other samples had one to two ounces or more of solidified fats in the test tubes, nearly filling two of them.

With a new national high of 600,000 heart attack fatalities, the American Heart Association urged people to reduce consumption of foods high in fat and cholesterol. People won't, of course, except for a wary few; for the latter, meat would be one of the first foods to avoid. Not only is there the emotional satisfaction of denying the meat industry its profits — however small a one-person protest may be — there is also the benefit to health. Supermarket-meat labels *USDA Choice* or *USDA Prime* really have nothing to do with the purity of the meat, but reflect the fat content; the meat with the greatest amount of fat is presented as the most desirable.

Sam Schmidt is not intent on disturbing the peace of Vero Beach in any loud ways; he is a quiet man, full of easy-going talk. Is he the real article, claiming no DES, a natural growing pace for his cattle, and low-fat meat that helps prevent heart disease? A skeptic, long-hardened by the many self-serving boasts dinning constantly in the American marketplace, might pass off Schmidt as another promoter. But there is a difference in him and his operation. Schmidt is there in his butcher shop every day, a live face over the counter, one the consumer can reach directly. Small towns know how to sniff out the frauds much easier than the big cities. Moreover, the local supermarkets in Vero Beach can easily supply the meat demands of the town, at least in quantity. But Schmidt's business thrives, suggesting that when the consumer has a chance to buy quality, he will.

On my last visit to Vero Beach, in January 1972, Schmidt had plans to enlarge his operation. He is convinced the time is right to offer the consumer organically-raised beef: no drugs, no artificial fertilizers or chemicals, no colorings, tenderizers or pesticides. "This is nothing revolutionary," he says modestly. "It's the way we farmed and raised cattle all along, before mechanization and chemical technology were put at the service of faster production and higher profits. I look like the odd man out, but in fact I'm the normal one. I'm raising cattle the way you'd do it if you cared more for your health than your convenience." Long ago, a businessman living and selling in his community was the basic of American commerce. That someone like Schmidt stands out from his fellow cattlemen is one measure of how far we have lapsed from that ideal.

Characters like Schmidt are scarcely a threat to the U.S. meat industry. Beef consumption per capita has risen from

63.4 pounds in 1950 to 115 pounds in 1972. The public is grumbling about meat prices, but Roswell Garst of Coon Rapids, Iowa — the gentleman farmer who was host to Nikita Khrushchev when he toured the heartlands in 1959 — has reassuring words. "Meeting a challenge is what farmers enjoy best," he wrote in May 1972 in the *New York Times.* "You can depend on having more beef — not suddenly — but steadily. Please don't be impatient — we will do our best." Not surprisingly, farmer Garst did not have a syllable to say about DES. He did not offer any warning to consumers that the meat industry was populated by many cattlemen and lobbyists who had little concern for the public's health. Instead, Mr. Garst said, "Be of good cheer. You are enjoying the finest diet that any people have ever enjoyed in history and the cost of the smallest per cent of your income that any people have ever experienced."

Lately Sam Schmidt has received visits from FDA inspectors who he believes are upset because of his advertising methods and his discussion within the community of the DES threat. Much of the Miami *Herald* piece had Schmidt talking about DES. By coincidence, the same time the FDA in Florida was coming in for "friendly visits" to the powerless Schmidt, FDA in Washington was counseling the public that "DES is clearly a useful and effective product." The strangeness of this view is that it came exactly when, in May and June 1970, new findings from the Department of Agriculture reported that DES was being found in cattle in increasing amounts. Dr. Charles C. Edwards, commissioner of the Food and Drug Administration, had said earlier that the rules on DES — moving the withdrawal time back to seven days from two days — would surely lower the rate of residues in meat. In the face of the new findings, Edwards backed away from protecting the citizens and instead called for public hearings on DES. These are needed, he said, if the FDA is to reach a "balanced and reasonable judgment" on the drug. Calling for a hearing — by proposing a formal action to withdraw the drug — had a bold ring to it, but it is often a means of delay. Hearings have been called on many other potentially hazardous drugs; months, sometimes years, pass before they are held. The Nixon Administration's talks about "the conquest of cancer" apparently did not allow doubts about a drug like DES that is a known carcinogen. The indecision of the agency had not gone unnoticed. Representative L. H. Fountain, a Democrat from North Carolina whose House Intergovernmental Relations Subcommittee oversees the FDA, said that Edwards "gave assurance in testimony in 1971 that he would ban DES if the government continued to find residues of the drug in one half of one per cent of the slaughtered animals sampled. Now that the stricter controls have been in effect for more than six months and DES is being found in 1.9 per cent of all animals sampled, it is incomprehensible to me that the commissioner would delay taking the action which he testified is required of him in these circumstances." The commissioner did delay, but finally, in August 1972, the FDA took action. It ordered an immediate halt in the production of cattle feed with DES and gave farmers until the end of 1972 to use the feed on hand.

Schmidt did not follow the debate in Washington closely. "Why should I?" he asks. "The meat I'm selling is not hoked-up, so there's no need for me to become an authority on loopholes. Besides, they can't drive me out of business. Too many people are tired of tasteless, chemicalized meat."

Tony Newcomb

IN THE LONG LISTS of America's great dreams, among the more persistent is the one of going back to the land. Bunched in by the city and its brutal contact sports, and believing there is no escape so they'd better adjust, perhaps fewer people have the longing today than twenty or thirty years ago. Then, one could listen to a parent or grandparent who had farmed tell tempting stories about gathering the crops or the goodness of the seasons and want to carry on the tradition of the plow. Now that we have disgraced the land, bungled our taste for nature, and grimly realize that our materialism may be doing us in, the man or woman who actually returns to the earth is perhaps the most valuable of all the purebreds still left.

Tony Newcomb, who owns and operates the Potomac Vegetable Farm, about twenty miles northwest of Washington where the Leesburg pike ribbons across the fertile uplands that lead to the Shenandoah Valley, is different from most other people who seem to be following a fashion. The latter go to the country to farm because that's what the *Whole Earth Catalog* says will make them happy, and never mind if you don't have a passion for farming. Newcomb is different because he has stayed with it.

I happened upon him and his farm by chance a few years ago when driving back from researching a story in West Virginia. Newcomb had built a small roadside stand, barely visible, as if he wanted only the true seekers to find it. I pulled in and filled the back seat with fresh corn, tomatoes, squash, beans, and other treasures that are hard to find in the city. Newcomb, tall, muscled, with small seams in his face from working outside, spoke easily about his farm. He admitted that when he first left Washington, there was a deep feeling of "Ah Wilderness!" to being out in the country, but that it soon passed. Newcomb gracefully resisted the man-of-the-earth role, yet what else is he? In Washington, he had worked for the government as a Bureau of the Budget economist, of all trades, but the instincts that led him out of the bureaucracy are the same ones that once urged John Muir, Johnny Appleseed, or Henry Thoreau to wander off from society and serve the earth in simplicity.

Newcomb represents a rare combination: a romantic dreamer who is doing well in a trade of harsh realities. He is modestly successful as a vegetable farmer, with earnings for the past two years totaling $15,000. But money is not the goal, nor is it much on his mind. "I think about other stakes," he said. "The personal satisfaction of it all, raising my family while I raise crops, listening to the earth's throb, knowing that the land is an ally, not an enemy." There is also the clean air he breathes, for which no antipollution law was needed, freedom from budget reports, print-outs, and other tediums of a government man, especially the one of taking orders from some big-desk mahatma. In brief, Newcomb had discovered that one of the goods of this earth is the earth itself.

As with most men who ride a wave, Newcomb does not brag about his luck. "A large part of farming," he said to me one afternoon while driving out to a far field where potatoes needed gathering, "is getting the breaks. I don't mean the farming by the corporations, these monsters of agri-business. But the kind by individuals. Getting good breaks means getting good weather, in finding and keeping a market, in hiring hearty workers who have some zeal for the land. This is what you need. You accept the good luck with gratitude and brace for the day when it might turn. Meanwhile, with your own hard work, you build up an equity — to fall back on — with nature."

Twelve years ago, when Newcomb and his wife Hui graduated from Oberlin College in Ohio, farming for a living was not in their plans. He came to Washington to do governmental economics and she chose to run a home, a vocation still precious to some women. In the spring of 1962, with an urge "to do a little gardening," Newcomb rented forty acres of land in Fairfax County and put himself to the test. He lost $4000. Unlike most fleeced tourists in strange lands, the Newcombs returned the next year. They broke even this time, learned a lot, and decided raising crops in the country was a better way to live than adding the government's numbers in the city.

"Every year," Newcomb says, "we have learned something — perhaps about planting, or rotating, marketing. And each year, the results are a little better. The tomatoes are lusher or the corn is larger. This is what I mean by personal satisfaction, an old term but still new to the emotions each time. I don't have to write a report about why my bottomlands were 'implemented' or get an audit to justify my tomatoes or write a grant proposal to plant corn. My only dialogue is with the earth — in the language of hard manual labor, the only tongue she listens to."

Newcomb starts talking in February. Tomatoes are planted in the greenhouse, to be nurtured during March and April, then set out in May and June. For other crops — corn, beans, squash, okra, peppers, beets, cucumbers, turnips — the land is tilled and the farm machinery is readied. Because he has a special reverence for both his land and the stomachs of his customers, Newcomb does not use organic phosphates, chlorinated hydrocarbons, or other chemicals to hype up the produce and fool the buyer. Insecticides and sprays are used cautiously, if at all. The farm is now 160 acres, most of it given over to corn and most of it rented land. "I don't see why more people don't leave the cities and farm," he said. "The speculators are just holding onto the land waiting for the population to creep out, and they will rent it cheaply. There's still so much of it."

One reason that Newcomb is now having good years is the long line of pleased consumers who eat his vegetables. They come to his stand fifty yards off the Leesburg pike and to six other stands in the county that buy his produce wholesale. Unlike many sellers who can hide from the consumer in board rooms guarded by customer-relations men, Newcomb has only one defense: the freshest and best products that the consumer's money can buy. That quaint idea was once a basic principle of American capitalism, but now only a few odd characters like Tony Newcomb dare work by it.

The competition facing Potomac Farms is formidable: large growers located on better soils with better irrigation surround Newcomb. But he wins out, or at worst ekes out, because he sells directly to the consumer through his own stand or the six he supplies. The produce is fresh and juicy. In contrast, supermarket vegetables are usually aging vegetables. Often a week or ten days passes from the time a product is picked, packed, shipped, shelved, and sold. In Newcomb's operation, the elapsed time is usually less than four hours.

One of the bitterest complaints among farmers today is the lack of workers. Often this is for good reasons — the pay is low, benefits are few, and little legal protection against exploitation exists. But the opposite is true for Newcomb. For the past few years, he has been flooded with job applications. Most of them are from college students seeking a wholesome summer in the sunlight, a feeling of community away from the cities and their madness. Most have no farm experience at the season's beginning; they can earn as much as $1000 from late June to early September. In a full-of-facts booklet meant to describe his farm to potential workers, Newcomb writes: "Often people unfamiliar with farming imagine that since much farm work is tedious, it also must be quite easy to learn, and that in a matter of hours anyone could be productive. The first few weeks of work are sobering, and for some, depressing."

I asked Newcomb what type of student works best. He smiled and stopped his truck between fields. "People with liberal views, politically and socially," he said, "are often not very physically industrious. They are reliable, honest, and fun to work with and are interested in learning about the work. They have first-week zeal. But they are easily bored by hard work day after day. Rising at daybreak, out to the fields with the dew, the high-noon rise of the sun, the long afternoon, and the dusk work of bringing things in — all this sounds idyllic when you're sitting in a dormitory room in January. But then doing it day after day, well, the liberals have trouble with this. Those with conservative or reactionary views are generally hard-working and filled with the Protestant work ethic. But they are not lighthearted and are often bores. They are a little doomlike about it all. The children of military parents tend to have acquired a distaste for manual labor which prevents their enjoying much of the work. But I have affection for all of the kids who come here. They have good hearts and I am refreshed by their innocence."

John Muir once expressed in his notes a thought which applies to Newcomb: ". . . If I should be fated to walk no more with Nature, be compelled to leave all I most devoutly love in the wilderness, return to civilization and be twisted into the characterless cable of society, then these sweet, free,

cumberless rovings will be as chinks and slits on life's hori-
zons, through which I may obtain glimpses of the treasures
that live in God's wilds beyond my reach." To many, that is
romantic gibberish. To others, like ex-Bureau-of-the-Budget
farmers, the chance to walk with nature is really a right —
as basic as free speech, and in these days, just as precious.

Charles Savage

ON THE ODD AND LONG CHANCE that a recent milk strike in Washington was harmfully affecting either the contentedness or production of some cows I knew, I took time off to visit them. Admittedly, the time I spent with Charles Savage and his herd of Holsteins was also a try at my own spiritual refreshment, because I returned to my office a little less convinced the planet is doomed as long as Mr. Savage and his cows are around. Muffled lows carried across the bottomlands as the cows — tall, deep-breathed, and spotted beauties — edged in near the gate that guarded the upslope pathway to the milking barn. The first autumn frost had yet to come, so the cows had been eating all afternoon the still-lush pasture grass. Sweat beaded like dew on their wide noses. The cows, steady ships anchored to routine, knew it was milking time and that soon someone would come over the ridge to lead them in.

Charles Savage, one of the last dairymen in Montgomery County, is a holdout against rising taxes and spreading developments. Every year, Mr. Savage can look out across his 275 acres in Gaithersburg, Maryland, and see another row of houses, drab look-alikes, going up on the edge of his property. They crowd in. His taxes in 1960 were $2000; in 1972 he paid nearly $4000. His herd produces about 2250 quarts daily. Mr. Savage says that "on paper it looks as if I'm rolling in clover. But after the dudes downtown get their share, I only get eleven cents a quart for my milk. Put that up against my two hundred and fifty dollars a month in land taxes, fifty dollars a month for personal property taxes, and a hundred dollars a month for insurance, and you can see that I'm in it for something else than money. I could easily sell my land to a developer, but I'm not going to give in."

Every day, a Lucerne tank-truck comes to take away a small sea of white gold. With the income from this, Mr. Savage has a safe port in the nationwide storm that is pushing many small dairymen off the land. His work is important. While many of the rest of us hold desperately onto the pommel of the saddle of urban-chaos, his contentment is that he rides free. He began thirty-one years ago with twenty dollars and since then has milked cows twice a day, all days of the week, through all seasons. Who does that anymore — at any kind of work? And still wants to continue?

I was relieved to learn during the first few minutes in conversation with Mr. Savage that his 325 registered Holsteins — 90 milkers, 200 heifers, and the rest dry, because they will be calving any day — are fine. The strike has not bothered them. Although my editor, who has more town than country instincts, said I couldn't possibly be serious in thinking that cows could be bothered by the in-fighting of a milk strike, I assured him I was. Having milked cows twice a day for five years, as well as shoveled tons of manure, helped deliver dozens of calves, nursed more than a few post-partum cows stricken with milk fever, delighted in the moos of lazy cows lowing across summer meadows, drunk a quart of rich, raw milk daily, and having come to understand the beasts' sacredness in India and wish it were so in America, I had firsthand, or better, first-finger, knowledge that getting a cow to give milk is not merely a matter of putting a pail under her udder and yanking.

A cow of fair perception can sense when something is not right in the milk world; she picks up the tension from the man or woman milking her. It may be sensed in a number of ways, the most common being when the milker rinses the cow's teats roughly, not gently, before the milking machine goes on. Since this touches the essence of the cow's femininity, as well as offends her professional dignity, she becomes emotionally upset. This would mean nothing — horses, cats, gerbils, and other animals are always getting emotionally upset at boorish treatment — except that the cow's sensitive milk-dropping glands are shut off. If done gently, with no tension caused by a milk strike, rinsing the cow's teats and udders stimulates the sucking thrusts of the calf, and thus gets the fullest measure of milk to drop. People who don't like cows say this only proves the animal's dumb, that she can be fooled into thinking an offspring is at the teat. My interpretation is different: the cow well knows about the gallons of white profit within her, but being the most idealistic of animals, she needs only a small sign of appreciation to produce.

By now, it was milking time. Mr. Savage was in the south corner of the barn attending to a nervous cow that he described as being a new member of the herd, two years and just freshened. Black and white swatched, as are all Holsteins, as compared to brown or brown and white Jerseys or Ayrshires, this cow had a nonsway, straight back and an upward, snob curve at the end of her nose. Below and to the rear was a tight derby-sized udder with long, alert teats that pointed in four directions, like guns out of a turret. When Mr. Savage finished, both man and beast seemed relieved. "Newcomers are a problem," he said. "It's all so strange to them. They've grown up getting special food and treatment, thinking they're entitled to it. Then one day, they come in here and have to get these machines hooked onto their teats. Quite a shock." Mr. Savage threw the dazed rookie a handful of molasses grain, and moved to the next cow. This was Miss Tycoon, much friendlier and much

older. He washed her teats, then gently put the four valves
of the machine on them, and patted her shank on the way up.
Miss Tycoon, a veteran cow, unfussed, with a low-slung udder
as soft as a grandmother's bosom and a supple nose that
twitched away three flies at once, appreciated the pat.

As with all cows in the Savage herd, Miss Tycoon eats
about 120 pounds of food daily: in hay, silage, and grain. In
return, she produces some 60 pounds of milk, or 30 quarts.
The herd population, or at least the producing part, is kept
near 90. These are the cream of the milk crop. Some 50
calves are raised a year, and about 20 cows are always in the
dry pasture ready for what the southern farmer calls birth-
ing. The herd, thanks to a happy bull and an artificial-semen
salesman, are kept in a constant state of pregnancy. Unlike
Jerseys which are smaller but produce milk with more butterfat, Holsteins are large, wide-hipped animals who produce
milk as though from an open tap. One of Mr. Savage's cows,
Miss Pride, a friendly mother with a loose-sway udder that
hangs like a full shopping bag, gave a record 33,840 pounds of
milk one recent year. With roughly one pint to one pound,
Miss Pride gave to the world nearly 17,000 quarts of milk.
Her sisters, aunts, and nieces in the Savage herd averaged
15,000 pounds, a figure that is well above the Maryland state
level.

While Mr. Savage was milking his cows, elsewhere in the
barn three farm hands were operating the other six machines. The barn itself was the old-fashioned stanchion type
where the cows walk up a middle aisle and take their places
in separate locks. The modern milking parlor has done
away with this, so that the cows come in singly to a raised
platform. They are milked and shooed out. It is hard to get
to know each cow that way, learn her quirks and manners,
and unless the milker is tall and the cow is short, hard to pat
any shanks. I have seen operations of both kinds, and the

cows in the stanchion setup always seem more peaceful, less jumpy. The pace is more leisurely, the cows can lean against the stanchion just far enough to lick each other's forehair — the origin of the term *cow lick* — and the herd identity is kept intact. There is nothing wrong with the raised-platform method — no herd rises in revolt — but it is not easy for the milk hand to keep a feeling of affection for the assembly-line cows.

"I suppose it's not so bad," says Mr. Savage, "but I have a hunch that the stanchion system gets more milk, even though the experts say you save money and time with the raised system. But the stanchions make sense. The cows are relaxed. They are with the others. No jostling. It's almost like a town meeting for them, without the speeches." One reason the cows may like stanchion is that they have the freedom of quirks. While we talked, Mr. Savage pointed to Miss Tycoon. Her quirk was always taking the stanchion nearest the mid-aisle separation, and none other. No one has ever figured out why, nor does anyone understand the quirks of several other Savage cows who habitually go to particular stanchions.

Hearing this reminded me of an unforgettable cow in the 100-member herd I milked in Conyers. Her name was Consideration, because next to milk that was the last thing anyone ever got from her. Her quirk was not taking the same stanchion every day, the way Miss Tycoon did, but taking a different one: going from one end of the barn to the other, day by day. I long thought that Consideration was abnormally fickle until I realized she was the only cow I knew who could count. That is what she was doing: practicing her numbers, starting with stanchion number one, then two, three, four, five, until she reached fifty, then back to number one. In time, Consideration had to go. She upset too many cows who had private stanchions and would not move for

anyone, not even a counting cow. Consideration was sold to
a man who wanted her as a family cow. The last I heard, he
changed her name to Numbers.

City school groups full of the children of asphalt and pavement who want to see "a real farm" often visit the Savage
herd. "Sometimes I get to talk with the teachers," said Mr.
Savage, who is fifty-five years old and few of them spent in a
classroom. "I'm worried about what's going on in some of
the schools. They train and teach the kids to become scientists, engineers, mathematicians, lawyers, professors, and
all that. The kids will come out overeducated, full of the-
ories and ideas. Meanwhile, who's taught them how to work,
and find satisfaction in it? Will they know how to shovel a
trench? Or lay out a fence? Or run a tractor over a spring-
time road? Of course, when I talk like this, the teachers get
nervous. They think I'm just a grumpy old farmer, stuck in
the past and anti-book learning. That's not it. I just think
that if we train everyone to do head work, a lot of the back
work won't get done. And what's worse, we'll begin to look
down on the back workers. They're menial, unworthy of us,
we with our fancy education. I wish the teachers would get
this across to the kids." Three of Mr. Savage's four sons own
their own herds of cows. All can dig trenches and mend
fences.

Among the thousands of words spilled like milk every year
solving the world's problems, I rarely see cows mentioned.
I can think of a number of groups whose members could
profit by a summer's worth of work around cows: the right-
wingers who oppose sex education in the schools because it is
Communist-inspired could learn that there is nothing at all
Marxist about a cow in heat and a bull in rut and nothing
harmful about Jimmy or Sally watching; the left-wingers
whose shoveling of manure would have a symbolic irony that
even they couldn't miss; the free spirits of the communes

who would learn the names of other grasses, like alfalfa, rye, corn, sorghum, clover; the greedy corporation men who would discover that milking a cow is not the same as milking the public, because the cow at least gets something in return. Finally, there is the group that shouldn't need prompting: the city-prisoned person whose lungs need a clearing out with farm air, whose eyes need to look long distances, whose soul needs reacquainting with sunrises, whose ears need to hear the melodious slurps of a calf on the teat, whose hands need to be torn away from the briefcase and put to the handle of a milking machine, persons whose spirits need relief from red lights, martinis, psychology, speeches, newspapers, causes, so that on return to these numbings, the memory of a few friendly cows at ease with nature will make it all bearable.

As winter moves in on Mr. Savage, much of the activity of his farm is getting in the final harvests of corn. Cows do not produce milk from good will but from good food. Already one silo was filled with corn, and combines worked the pastures in a steady hum while the daylight lasted. On learning that he has done this kind of work every day for thirty-one years, city visitors often ask Mr. Savage why he isn't exhausted. "Why should I be?" he answers. "The earth renews itself, and so do the people who work it." He smiles at the irony that many of those who pose this question about exhaustion are themselves bushed — from battling traffic, the boss, the politicians.

It is tempting to romanticize farm life, singing only the high notes in the hymn to its workers and cows. "Ah, wilderness!" says the weekend visitor; if he stayed longer, perhaps it would be "Ugh, wilderness!" The animals, the earth, the repairs — all these need attention, and to those used to the tastes of urban delight, it can be a dry diet. But it fills. One reason, at least in Mr. Savage's case, is that although he makes money at his work, no one hands him a pay envelope for it. Instead, he is free to measure his own worth, deal in his own currencies, and take profits from the treasures that the rest of us might be passing up: pure air, unhurried days, respect for the land and the company of generous, gentle cows. Especially them.

PART V
Clairfield May Make It

The Huddlestons

Misery voyeurs, eastern weeklies, and TV camera crews still come to Appalachia to express or excite outrage at the poverty of tired, tattered and gaunt, blank-eyed mountain people; but they no longer flock in or stream in. The nation has tired of Appalachia, the way it has tired of the Peace Corps, the SCLC, and migrant workers. As for many of the Appalachian poor, or at least most of the few thousand scattered around a remote valley in Clairfield in northeast Tennessee, it is almost as if there was never an OEO or HEW, never a social worker in from over the mountains to "help," never an Appalachian Regional Commission with high promises.

Clairfield is about two hours north of Knoxville, or twenty crossed-over Cumberland Mountains, on the bottom rim of Appalachia and the bottom of nearly everything else. It once had a population of over 20,000, as late as fifteen years ago when its mountains were treasures of coal and lumber, and manpower was the only way the companies could plunder them. But the deep mines have been closed, someone beyond the mountains has gotten rich; now the coal is being strip-mined, so someone else in Pittsburgh, New York, or Charleston can get rich.

Precisely because the outward effects of poverty in Appalachia are so measurable, the region has attracted, since John Kennedy's 1960 West Virginia, large numbers of outside theorists. Many of the more serious ones have been willing to leave their towers for a year or two, come live in the mountains with the people, and bring on social change that way. But because *change* is an eastern word, from a place of speed, many have been temperamentally ill-suited for the mountains, where change is slower. The pacing is different and the mountain people refuse to jump up and down in glee whenever a new savior comes in saying he knows just what needs to be done.

The only outsider who has come into Clairfield in recent years and stayed is Marie Cirillo. In her early forties, wary of federal big-talkers and sensitive to mountain voices, she spent fifteen years as a sister in the Catholic order of Glenmary Sisters. Some years ago, when the order clumsily refused to give a group of innovative sisters the freedom to try new styles in their work, forty-four out of sixty-one left. They formed a group which continued to work in the mountains, but without pressure from bossy reverend mothers or bishops. Occasionally, Marie Cirillo came to Washington for grant hunting. I met her by chance in 1967 when she was making the rounds. In the past five years, at her invitation, I have made three visits to Clairfield to try to understand the valuable mountain culture and get close to its people. I thought it was better to know one community well than know several on the surface.

The sociologists, who are master measurers and have Appalachia down cold, call the hollows in places like Clairfield *depressed areas.* On the charts it may read like that, but in the middle of the summer flush, there is nothing depressing in sight; nature has been too generous for that. In mid-July, the air is shot with rich earth odors, carrying the smells of muskrat castor, and pines and persimmons that pile down the mountains and cut away only for roads and streams. Jays flash and scream in the bushes, their beaks blue-red with the stains of checkerberries and blackberries. Dervishes of wildlife — lizards, foxes, voles, bull rabbits — track noiselessly through the brush. Driving up looping hollow roads that billow with dust the color of orange talc, you come to a knoll where you can see, far off and through a glass clearly, the hazed purple folds of the Great Smokies.

Living in scenes similar to these are Steely Huddleston, Pauline, his wife of thirty years, and his brother Jim. Their cabin — beyond the mountains, the irreverent would call it a shack or a shanty — has no running water, heat, or electricity, has a six-and-a-half-foot ceiling, a tin and tarpaper roof above, with chickens and rattlesnakes occasionally in the underpinning below. It is five miles, deep in a hollow, from Clairfield. My visit to the Huddlestons took place during the week of the first moonshot in July 1969. Nothing about this nonsense interested me, except to keep count of the tax money being wasted without anyone checking with the taxpayers to find out whether they wanted it wasted this way. There was no point in staying around Washington because the papers and television were full of moon talk, as flat as two mirrors facing each other. More would be happening among the craters of Clairfield, I thought, a place nearly as desolate as any lunar-module landing site. I already knew more about the layout of the moon than the layout of Clairfield. "Come down," said Marie Cirillo." I want you to meet the Huddleston brothers."

The front porch, where the Huddlestons gather in the evening or take a chair break when a rare visitor shows up, gives onto a patch where sweet Williams, tiger lilies, hydrangeas, asters, and a row of Winesap apple trees are full-blooming in July. Out back are a mule, a bull, two Jersey milk cows, one hound, and fourteen Chinese geese. In the summer, the animals roam free, pecking or grazing where the food is; wintertime, they stay in log pens and sheds. In the family's garden, potatoes, cabbage, lettuce, corn, cucumbers, beets, and muskmelons are grown.

The steady tragedy in the Huddlestons' life, aside from

the numbing one of poverty that forces them to live on a ninety-dollar old-age-assistance check, is the small mountain of coal slag in their front yard. In 1965, a British land-grant company, oddly called the American Association, decided to strip-mine the mountainside facing the Huddleston cabin. With the kind of arrogance and cruelty that corporations can dish out when the victims are not seen face to face, the company went after its coal and piled the left-over slag, gooey mud and dirt, almost onto the Huddlestons' front porch. Before long, the heap stretched a mile and rose to 200 feet. Aside from the damage done to their souls — mountains are in the souls of Appalachians, and to destroy one is to destroy the other — the enormous slag pile covered over the Huddlestons' well, two springs, a fruit basement, a trail, and the view. It also drove away the rabbits, squirrels, and deer. The stripper took away a mountain of nature and replaced it with a mountain of black garbage. Occasionally, in other parts of the mountains, the people fought back and blocked the plundering by the companies, but mostly these were rare citizen groups aided by lawyers. The Huddlestons had no lawyer, nor did they have neighbors to form an association of protest. They had no choice but to genuflect before the gods atop the Mt. Olympus slag pile, all the while paying homage to the secret faith they believed in long before the coal company came. They did not adjust within.

As with many who have a deep religion, the Huddlestons showed their surface personalities first. This was my second visit to them, the earlier one having been in 1967. They remembered me. Gently, with smiles, they greeted me by joking about my clothes. Steely was glad to see that I wasn't wearing a tie on this visit. He could see no reason, he said, for putting a rope around one's neck, especially in the mountains when it could catch on a limb and choke a man. "He's learning," said brother Jim, nodding in my direction and then breaking into a leathery grin. Steely asked me where I'd been since visiting the Clear Fork Valley the year before. I said California, New York, Florida, Texas, all over. "I've been all over, too," he said, standing in the doorway of the same cabin he lives in now and from which he has never traveled more than a few miles. "I've been down to the creek for water every other day. I've gone to fetch a calf when it was born back in the birch cluster. I've been to the outhouse a lot [laughter from Pauline and Jim]. I've walked up and down my gardens at least a thousand miles planting and picking. So I've been all over, too."

Although the Huddlestons play their portable radio mostly for the mountain music, and then only in evenings before a 9 p.m. bedtime, they knew about the moon voyage. The voyage upset them. At first, they talked around their "botheration," not coming out directly with their feelings. I sensed they didn't wish to be rude to me. For all they knew, I might have been dazzled silly by the idea of men landing on the moon, and, like good hosts, would not want to lower my high moment. But I told the Huddlestons that I wasn't dazzled at all by the moon business; I came from Washington to the mountain community of Clairfield precisely to get away from the fever the moonshot was raising at that time among friends of mine who normally keep their heads. To me, the space program was a waste of precious government money — meaning the people's money — that should have been flooded to dry-well places like central Appalachia. This was the straight liberal line, but I assumed it was fresh to the Huddlestons. So they listened to me criticizing the moon business — what a shame to spend so much money with so little return, what an insult to the poor. My knees were jerking to my own arguments.

I thought by now that Steely would see we were both on the same antimoon side, and he would fall in with my think-

ing. But he surprised me, the way country men with the natural force of honesty behind them can cause surprise among
urbans. "None of that bothers me," said Steely, "although
we need money here. Badly, all the time. The reason I don't
like men going to the moon is because that's not where men
belong. The Lord doesn't want them there. Do you remember in the Old Testament when they tried to build a tower
so high that it would reach heaven? Remember what happened? It fell on them. They were killed by the Lord. He
didn't want them messing." Steely quoted the lines from
Genesis: "And they said, come, let us build a city and a tower,
whose top may reach unto heaven; and let us make a name."
Although Genesis does not literally say the tower fell on the
people, many have since believed it did.

Steely's application of the Babel story to the moon voyage
was a new one to me then, and I have heard no one offer it
since. Doubtlessly, it would strike many of the best liberals
as incredible that one of the poorest persons in Appalachia,
who would starve if he didn't rise at dawn to tend his crops
and whose material goods are either nonexistent or wearing
out, did not see the moon landing the way they do: as a poor
ordering of the much discussed national priorities. To
Steely, it was not a question of politics or economics, but one
of spirituality. He believed that when God wants men to
inhabit other planets, rockets will not be used. "The Lord,"
he insisted, "can take us to the moon or the sun in the next
life, if it suits Him. But it's not for us to decide now."

Wanting to cut away any Holy Joe fat that might seem to
be encasing the meat of his Biblical argument, Steely said
he also had a practical reason for insisting that men stay on
the earth. "The moon is important for my crops. Moonlight helps them grow at night, the way sunlight stretches
them in the day. How do we know what walking on the
moon will do to our light power? I say we shouldn't tamper

with the way the Lord set up things. What happens to my crops if they don't get the right moonlight on them?"

The conversation drifted to other things: the apple tree struck by lightning in the spring and how the fruit is growing puny as a result; the rattler which had recently taken Steely by surprise (laughter from Pauline and Jim) but which he managed to kill with a stick; the flower seeds Pauline hung in a tobacco pouch over the door to dry out; the protective Chinese goose that hisses strangers away from the sleeping hound. On leaving the Huddlestons and thanking them for both the afternoon and the invitation to come back again — "Don't wait for another blame moonshot," they said — I would have liked to have had them as allies in the debate about "national priorities" then going on. After all, they were the true poor and many outsiders had lined up on *their* side. But unlike many of those outsiders who are crowded into liberal, moderate, or conservative camps, as if life is reduceable to that, the Huddlestons are not for sale, no matter the cause.

They are quiet people, who work hard at manual labor and get weary. They endure the pains of a private hell so intense that not even sharing it will give them a little relief. So they keep it to themselves, which, at least in the mountains, is a way of holding on to one's integrity. That is important if you are going to live on the land, among the mountains, through the seasons, beaten down by one kind of life, but rising out of naked necessity to a greater life.

Bobby Loveday

ALTHOUGH MANY OTHER TOWNS in Appalachia have been able
to rejoin affluent America, Clairfield, Tennessee, hasn't.
Whether it suffers only a case of temporary hard luck or is
permanently sunk in poverty is not known for now. The
mountains are divided by the planners into growth and nongrowth areas, and Clairfield is decidedly in the second. The
only sure fact about Clairfield, and hundreds of other towns
like it, is the cause of its poverty: years ago, someone decided to get rich on it, and corporational economy backed by
institutionalized power said, "Go ahead and get rich, it will
help us too." The destruction of Clairfield was bloodless and
noiseless. The men of money and power never knew the war
games they were in on. That, more than the destruction
itself, is the real tragedy of Clairfield because it means that
poverty in Appalachia is still an Appalachian problem, not
an American problem. The people who can solve it are unaware they caused it, but there is still the chance that local
people will find a way out themselves.

One way out, totally hopeless, was offered by an ex-miner I
talked with one afternoon. I asked him what he thought
about the American government's spending $870 a year
per person in Vietnam but only $58 for the poor in America.
He scratched his chin and said, "I don't know how to get to
Vietnam but I ought to go there." Another way, totally
hopeful, is the idea that eliminating poverty in Appalachia
cannot be only a political or an economic process, it must
also be a personal process. It must move forward by the en-

ergy of the mountain people themselves. If community or-
ganizing was once the main smelling salts by which a near
dead Appalachia would be revived, setting up an industry
has now joined it.

On my first two stays in Clairfield, little of what was happening — a new softball league, a summer folk festival, talk
of a newspaper — promised to bring any money into Clairfield. The small town of 500, with its off-shoots of wornout
hollows, had endured all the known ills of mountain poverty,
and then some. Unemployment was 30 per cent, the once
beautiful mountains rimming the valley were gashed by strip
mines, the creek bed was befouled by acid runoff, large numbers of the young had fled by thumb or by Greyhound. Many
of the elderly were scraping by on food stamps, black-lung
money, or pensions, and half the people had incomes under
$2000. Under it all, low like a coal seam, are the poor spoken
of by Richard Margolis who "live under the delusion that the
nation's leadership does not know they are suffering. If the
leaders knew, they would do something about it, wouldn't
they?" On my third visit, though, despite an experience of
nothingness that remained with many of the people, there
was talk that change might be coming.

In pride and amazement, they referred to the new factory
in town. It was the first industry ever for Clairfield — after
coal — and the people got it with no research and demonstration grants from the government, no cash from the highway-
happy Appalachian Regional Commission, and no lobbying
from a trade association in Washington. The story of the new
Clairfield Pallet Factory may be seen as the last gasp of a
dying town or as the first breath of one pulsating to life again.
The latter is the view in Clairfield. Either way, the community is in touch with the oldest of emotions, making an
honorable living with one's hands.

The factory, opened in the spring of 1971, produces pallets. A pallet is a wooden device used as a portable platform for handling, storing, or hauling materials and packages in factories, warehouses, and trucks. Much of American industry literally leans on pallets. Following the formation of the local Model Valley Industrial Development Council in 1967 — begun by a few citizens of hope and three hundred dollars — the group speculated on what industry Clairfield could get into. Unlike in the bureaucracies of Washington, speculation is not an endless occupation in the mountains, so the subject was dropped when no answer suggested itself and nothing happened. Three years later, Brady Deaton, a professional economist and former Peace Corps volunteer, heard about Clairfield by chance and came to town as a fellow of the Robert F. Kennedy Memorial Foundation.* The economist studied the market possibilities from within the region itself and suggested pallets. They could be made from local timber preserves, they required little heavy machinery beyond a sawmill, which a local lumberman was already running, and some firms within a 300-mile area were in need of pallets.

One of those in the community who believed Clairfield's bootstrap could be pulled up was Bobby Loveday. Born and raised in the valley, Loveday is one of the few young people who made a conscious choice to stay. He is thirty-six, easy-mannered, and has a powerful, silent strength. He doesn't defend his town and its mountains, but he talks with excitement about the factory and how it is already a symbol that a future lies in Appalachia. "It's coming to us if we can only hold out to still be here when it arrives," he said. "I worry about this a little, that we'll forget the value of what we have here in the mountains. I lived in Detroit

* Marie Cirillo told me that Brady Deaton had seen a story of mine in 1969 that ran in the Milwaukee *Journal*, as carried by the Washington *Post*–Los Angeles *Times* Wire Service. The story said that Clairfield was looking for an economist. Mr. Deaton wrote to Marie Cirillo, and from that he eventually came to the community.

for three months and I saw the stars at night only once. I don't mean that I never went outdoors. I did. But the soot in the air — it blocked the view. You couldn't see through it, it was so thick. Like clouds. Here in the mountains, which I came back to fast, nature is the same now as it was one hundred years ago. People used to call this area the backwoods but now they're seeing that back in the woods is the place to be. Nature is here. So is the future. Maybe a lot of our streets aren't paved, like the wide avenues of the cities. But our air is clean. What would you rather have — dirty lungs or muddy shoes? I'll take the muddy shoes. I can clean them every night."

With an original investment of $21,000, construction of the factory was begun by Loveday and a small crew. The structure was corrugated steel, in a low-roofed style the size of two tennis courts end to end. Production began in July 1971. Currently, the contracts are moderate to good. One load averaging 400 pallets is shipped every week to a Westinghouse plant in Abingdon, Virginia. Loveday said the shipment was expected to triple soon. The projected wages for the first year were $53,000, with a product value of $60,000. The workers earn $72 a week, before taxes. "Few of us in Clairfield had much experience in any kind of industrial work," Loveday said one afternoon. "But when word got around that a pallet factory would get started, we had at least fifty applications for work." Twelve men were eventually chosen. The council applied for, and received, a state on-the-job training program in which wages of $1.70 an hour were paid in equal shares by the council and the state. According to Loveday, the training program had the best attendance record and lowest drop-out rate in Tennessee that year.

By the summer of 1972, the pallet factory was off to a fair start, but Loveday was saying that a second thrust was needed if long-haul success was to come. A main struggle, he believed, was keeping an inventory. Pallets are made in various sizes, so the problem is having sufficient timber that is close to the actual size of the projected pallet. That way there is little or no waste of timber — often the measure of profit. During the first year of operations, the timber that did not end up in pallets had to be paid for anyway. Loveday and the council began looking around for money possibilities — from a foundation, sale of stock, private philanthropy — that would enable them to buy the sawmill equipment for about $3500. They would then be able to cut their own wood to whatever sizes were needed for a particular order, rather than having the wood cut in only general sizes. "We have the problem all businesses must eventually face," says Loveday. "We need money to make money."

One reason investors tend to stay clear of places like Clairfield is the fact that it is a part of nongrowth Appalachia. This is true: the town is far from a major highway, is cut off by mountains from the money flow of the county seat at Tazewell, and the coal pickings have long been slim. But it is not easy to forget that although the town may be nongrowth — which is only an accident of geography — the people are not. They are the opposite, refusing adjustment with both the popular view of mountain people as resigned and slow and the idea that help must come from outside, not inside, the mountains. The workers at the pallet factory see themselves growing in a way no one imagined a few years ago. The growth is not dramatic perhaps — the way boom towns used to appear overnight in Appalachia when coal was discovered — but nevertheless it is present. Running a small business — making it work and making sense from it all — is still one of the main connections Americans have to their past. No one told Bobby Loveday or any of the people of Clairfield this. They discovered it themselves: the steady idea that the past is the future.

Save Our Cumberland Mountains

STINKING CREEK, TENNESSEE, is a few hollows over from Clairfield. Its name, the stories say, comes from a summer day in the early twenties when a mountain farmer, too tired to dig a hole, heaved the carcass of his dead cow into the creek bed near his bottomlands. On a windless day, the stench from the decaying corpse hung over the hollow. But it disappeared when the creek carried off the late Bessie. With mountain humor, the coursing waterway became known as Stinking Creek. In the 1920s, old-timers recall, it was a clear and fresh stream, lively with pure water, good for drinking and washing, and especially fine for fishing. The creek was a community institution, a stethoscope put to the heart of the community as a way of hearing the pulse of the mountain culture. What was a funny name for the parents and grandparents of the people now living along Stinking Creek is for today's people a wretched tragedy. Today, Stinking Creek is truly a stinking creek. The fish are long gone, so is the insect and fauna life. Acid runoff from the strip mines has poisoned the water, blackening it and forcing the air out. No farmer today would ever use the creek as a cattle graveyard the way that anonymous farmer did forty years ago; the dead would be disgraced.

My first visit to Clairfield came during the entertainment of the moonshot and my most recent visit coincided with another stagey affair — Nixon's China trip. When this came around, in early 1972, Washington again showed signs of inhaling deep the ether of a Great Event; so while the news-

papers and news shows went into the deep sleep of reporting
Nixon's every banal word, it was time to duck away to the
back hollows around Clairfield. In 1968, I found no one who
thought the moonshot was worth noticing and, in 1972, the
same wisdom prevailed because no one cared about Peking.
To the mountain people, both events were theater — and
nothing is wrong with that — but they had other dramas,
closer to life, to watch.

On a February afternoon, bleak with cold drizzle and the
blur of low-hung clouds, Jimmy Sands was driving through
the Cumberland Mountains to his home in the hollows of
Duff, about ten miles from Clairfield. He pulled to the side
of the mucky road and told me to look at the sad, ghastly but
now common sight: a strip-mined mountain. It loomed 100
yards across Stinking Creek. "It's a murdered mountain,"
Sands said, nodding to the corpse of earth. Sands, thirty-two,
a short man with reddish hair springing with an easy flow
from his scalp, is a free-lance carpenter. Some front teeth are
missing — vacant emblems of a childhood by Nehi soft drinks
— but he smiles nonetheless. He has had hard luck in his life,
but the piece he is least adjusted to is the strip mining. He
and his wife own a few acres of lonesome land far back in
Duff, but the quiet has been shattered by the dynamite blast-
ing of the strippers and the noisy ravaging of the power shovels. A tiny creek ran a few yards off from the Sands' home but
the bulldozers wiped it out completely. Sands had never
seen or heard of anything like it. "It was just gone one morning," he said. "Made into a mud heap. I didn't know people
could do things like that. I didn't even know they would
want to."

The mountain behind Stinking Creek was one of hundreds in the area that the coal companies had gouged for the
black gold. To get at a coal seam in the mountain, the strip
miners had dynamited, bulldozed, and scooped into the

mountain's natural growth of soil, trees, shrubs, flowers, and plant life. The played-out land becomes a wide swath of rocks, sludge, gunk, disheveled trees, and useless soil. It may be hard for the urban imagination to picture a strip-mined mountain, but an idea can be had on why so many in the mountains resent the destruction: what if one morning commuters along Rock Creek Parkway or George Washington Memorial Parkway — to take two of the scenic routes into the nation's capital — saw those precious hills a rubble of slop and dirt, and were informed a coal seam had been found? How would we feel about it? Of course, the National Coal Association would tell us that the coal was needed because national security was at stake and that we were on the verge of a power crisis. (Never mind the high tonnage we ship to Japan.) But would the grim sight be any less painful because of that guff?

If the land of Campbell County is insulted, so are many of the citizens, especially people like Sands, who won't stay quiet. Campbell ranks among the poorest per family in income but among the richest minerally. Many in the mountains live with this irony because, first, they feel powerless to change a system kept almighty by local politics and outside money, and second, because in rocking the boat, you yourself may be washed overboard. Sands doesn't share these views, nor does anyone else in a citizens' group formed in early 1972 called Save Our Cumberland Mountains. SOCM (pronounced "sock 'em") is a group of mountain people from a five-county area that includes Campbell, Claiborne, Morgan, Scott, and Anderson. Because Appalachia has little tradition for citizen campaigns or public movements — rural isolation is one reason, personal reticence about scene-making is another — the formation of the group in itself was unusual. Its purpose is to improve life in the mountain areas in northeast Tennessee, mostly by saving the moun-

tains and homeland against the strip miners. At their meetings, held in tiny mountain churches or abandoned union
halls, the members try to rouse each other's confidence and
heart.

Millard Branam of White Oak, not far from Duff, told his
brothers and sisters one night, "The problem I see is getting
people to realize just what is really happening to our country and what we are dealing with when we are dealing with
the coal companies. We know they are just out to make
money. We have a fight on now. Right now, I think we have
a good start and it's no time to let up. We should work
harder to get people in this area to see what we are working
for. You don't have to live right in the strip pits to be hurt.
If you live away from the destruction you are hurt just as
bad as us people that live right in it. These mountains belong to all of us. Our water is getting so bad that you can
hardly drink it, and our roads have ruts until you can hardly
drive over them. I think we should have a meeting once a
month in our community to discuss our problems and try to
get new members. We have a strip-mine law. We don't know
what it is worth yet. If we let up now, that's what the companies want. We should keep moving and try to get a better
law. We are all in this fight we should have started years
ago. But it's not too late. I think we have a whole lot to
gain and plenty of mountains to lose if we don't stop this
stripping. There is one thing I would like to say. It's good
to know we have people that care for where we live to try to
practice it. We may be small in numbers, but we can show
our state and nation we do care enough to try to save it."
This kind of brave talk has seldom been heard in the region,
and the audiences are a little stiff when listening to it. They
applaud with mild claps, as though embarrassed by the
emotions.

SOCM would rank as just another band of little people

biting like gnats against the hide of corporate giants, but some members of the group had the sense to begin their battle not with the usual weapon of polemics, which seldom wins anything, but with facts. In the summer of 1971, a group of Vanderbilt University students began a research project that examined such obscurities as courthouse records, state tax laws, and county mineral and land studies. This was hardly the exciting work of social reform, but it was necessary work. That so few have been willing to endure its tedium is one explanation of why the coal companies have had a free hand and a freer shovel to plunder the mountains. After gathering their facts, the SOCM group said that "one important reason for the local poverty in northeast Tennessee is that virtually all of the coal wealth is controlled by a few, large outside corporations which reap handsome profits on royalties from coal operations, yet escape local taxation, in violation of state law, because the coal has not been assessed as part of the property value. Although these large companies own over 33 per cent of the land area of these five counties, they accounted for less than 4 per cent of the property tax revenue in 1970."

The students canvassed the five counties, explaining house by house the facts they uncovered in the records. The citizens well knew the breaking-and-entering tactics of the coal industry, but the details of the thievery had always been a mystery. Soon after, a citizens' complaint — filed by 400 taxpayers in the five counties — charged that the Tennessee State Board of Equalization had failed to tax the vast coal resources in a manner required by law. As a result, the group said in the complaint, their counties were losing several hundred thousand dollars yearly in uncollected property taxes. Thus, the small, nonmineral landowner has been forced to carry an unfair burden for schools, roads, hospitals, and other social needs. Obviously, the burden has been too heavy in

many cases; in hollows like Stinking Creek, Duff, White
Oak, and the others around Clairfield, either no schools or
roads exist at all or they are tumble-down ones and wornout. "People come in from outside," said Jimmy Sands after
the complaint was filed, "and tell us we shouldn't agitate.
That's not the mountain way of doing things. Besides that,
life isn't fair, they tell us. Well, the fact is, life is fair. The
tax assessor isn't."

The director of the State Board of Equalization is Freeley
Cook. He is a long-time statehouse bureaucrat, with a sailor's
eye for not making waves. He had little to say about the
complaint, except to insist that it was only a complaint and
not a legal suit, and that he, Freeley Cook, was running the
show, "not these Vandy students." He told me in an interview that his office had held a hearing on the complaint and
was now "assisting the local county tax assessors in studying
the mineral values of the land" to see if more money should
be coming in. Cook offered no comment on whether the
companies had been gypping the tax men in the counties, nor
did he dare suggest that the local assessors might not care
if they were gypped, since the operators were strong and it
was only tax money anyway. The citizens'-group lawyer was
Gilbert Merritt of Nashville, a former U.S. district attorney
for middle Tennessee and known in the region for his low
toleration of guff. Merritt believed that "the local county
tax assessors just haven't been doing their job, even though
it's clear the law requires them to. For one thing, the coal
operators have a cordial relationship with the assessors, who
are elected officials. As a legal proposition, I don't think the
citizens' suit is contestable. It's a question of time when the
taxes will be equalized."

Although the voices of these Cumberland people are a
new sound in Appalachia, they join a chorus elsewhere calling out for tax equalization. Ralph Nader, as usual ahead of

everyone else, has been thinking about it for years. He wrote, in a February 1972 piece in the *New Republic* called "The Property Tax Gyp," "In the coal regions of Appalachia, the coal companies, although already enjoying federal depletion allowances, present their own assessments to most tax commissioners. Even if a commissioner wants to check the figures, he lacks the technical know-how and the backing of his superiors, who are often tied to the coal industry. Self-assessment by the highly profitable coal companies drains millions of dollars from the coal-rich but revenue-starved mountain counties with their impoverished school systems. Acres of coal land conservatively worth $200 to $500 per acre are assessed at $10 per acre. Other large coal acreages have not even been reported to all the assessors."

Getting a better tax break may one day ease the poverty in the five counties, but whether or not the people will ever get back their mountain valleys and streams is another question. This is a major goal of SOCM: to ban strip mining in Tennessee. "Large landowners from New York, Connecticut, and Illinois and a few local strip-mine operators gain the benefits," the group said in one of their early written statements, "while Tennessee pays the cost in the form of a ruined environment, stunted economic development, and higher taxes in the future to 'reclaim the mountains' . . . The Tennessee coalfield is spotty and erratic; its seams are thin compared to those in other Appalachia states. Land in the Cumberlands is not best suited for stripping. It should be saved for recreation, industry, game and forest preserves."

SOCM had been trying for a year to show the state's politicians what was happening in northeast Tennessee, and in that way inspire them to replace Tennessee's weak and poorly enforced strip-mine law. Always, the politicians were too busy with matters of state, but they would certainly "study the problem."

A few weeks before I visited Clairfield, a Senate subcommittee made a field trip to the stripping sites. Two senators came — Bellmon of Oklahoma and Moss of Utah — but they toured by helicopter and never muddied their shoes. Nor did they meet with citizens like Jimmy Sands who are the victims of the stripping and should at least have had a word with the mighties from Washington. But Bellmon and Moss did have a pleasant chat with a strip-mine operator who told about his reclamation efforts and how beautiful the land could be made after the coal mountains were ripped apart. Apparently, the high-standing senators were impressed because they returned to Washington saying that reason and moderation was called for regarding legislation and that more study was needed.

The only politician who cared enough about the victims in east Tennessee to come see them was Fred Harris. He was then a senator from Oklahoma, a restless, blunt man who had little use for the pointless antics of the Congress. Marie Cirillo loaned her car to Jimmy Sands, who drove Harris around the mountain roads; I caught a ride with them. Harris spent a full day going through the hollows looking at the devastation. This was his first trip and it reminded him a little of Vietnam. "The stripping is shocking, there's no denying that, but it's fitting in a grim kind of way. There we are in Vietnam, defoliating the land, a few million bomb craters caused by us and a total of one sixth of the earth environmentally ruined. We do it there, so why not do it here? We have the knack." Many in the mining towns around Clairfield had never heard of a politican who said strip mining should be banned totally — as Harris said to everyone he met — so he was well received, often with embraces and tears. Harris was a novelty for another reason: a few people in the hollows had seen a live politician before but none could recall a visit from one who wasn't running for office and grubbing for votes. After a day of traveling around, having lunch with a mountain family, slogging through the mud, going into the scars of the mountains, Harris said that he supported more strongly than ever the legislation proposed by Representative Ken Hechler of West Virginia. Among other strictnesses, the bill would ban strip mining within six months of enactment. "It's the same as setting a date on pollution for cars," Harris said. "If you keep compromising, you'll never get around to it. To stop strip mining, a sixth-month deadline is absolutely necessary. Unless you apply this kind of pressure on the corporations, they'll never stop. Why should they? There's also the incentive to look for new ways of getting our energy — such as going back to deep mining. Meanwhile, it's wrong to tear up the land for profit."

Harris's day was mostly a boring one, except for learning about the people and seeing the destruction of the timbered hills. But lively action did break at one point. SOCM, doing smart advance work, arranged a meeting between Harris and a group of local strip miners in Lake City. When Harris, Sands, and the others walked into the meeting room, one of the strippers asked why the senator hadn't come. Another one, looking at me in a tie, thought I was the senator. Small wonder they missed Harris. He wore cowboy boots, by now well muddied, a toboggan cap, a sloppy mustache, and a windbreaker jacket. Finally convincing them that he was indeed a U.S. senator, Harris sat down with the group. "I just came through land in Campbell County that some of you have stripped and it's just a goddamned scandal," Harris began, every inch the statesman. There was a low gasp from one of the strippers, and the same one who thought I was the senator now looked at me again wishing I were; anyone would be better than this unruly character from Oklahoma. Present at the meeting, besides Harris and the SOCM members, was Dexter Rains, head of the Tennessee Land and

Mine Company, Dane Miller of the Arnold Coal Company, Richard Spectnagle of the Tennessee Company, and A. E. Funk of the American Association, the same firm that devastated Steely and Jim Huddleston's front yard in Clairfield. Funk did most of the talking, with the others nodding in agreement.

"American Association," he said, "for which I work and am a stockholder, owns eighty thousand acres and we've been stripping for twenty years. I'm satisfied that our stripping is eighty-five per cent correct, but we sometimes have bad operators who don't reclaim properly some fifteen per cent of the land they strip. We fire them. We lease our lands, so others do the stripping." Harris told Funk that he had been throughout most of Campbell County that day and had seen no reclaimed site. He told the operators that they were typical of what America didn't need — big corporations that get "richer and richer and the poor growing poorer and poorer. You coal operators take the natural resources out, but how can you explain why the schools and the roads I saw were so inadequate?" Funk said, "Everyone wants to hurry up and start reclaiming, but it takes four to five years. Nature will take care of it. The natural vegetation will reappear." He acknowledged to Harris that "maybe we pollute the streams a little" but this is caused by "some bad operators. I'm sorry if you don't like what it looks like." Harris angrily argued back about the greediness of people like those in Funk's company. Standing back against the wall, Jimmy Sands smiled widely, almost in daze of happiness at what he was hearing from Harris. "Just what do you want of us?" Funk asked tersely. Harris replied that for a start he'd like to look at some of the reclaimed sites that Funk and the other kept boasting about. "Just show me one," said Harris, "and I'll report to the Senate on the good work you're doing." His offer was not taken.

Not everyone in the mountains agrees that stripping should be banned. Aside from many politicians — local and national ones who believe that the strip-mine industry knows best or that if controls are needed they should be "reasonable" — a group called Save Our Jobs was formed in Campbell County. A few weeks before my visit, a rally was held. The Campbell County *Times* in nearby La Follette reports that "miners, various representatives of heavy-equipment companies and others interested in the welfare of the industry took the speaker's stand to warn that sharp restrictions or stoppage of strip mining will cause many jobs to be lost and have dire effects on the economy of the area." Citing bad publicity, long-haired students, university professors, and outside trouble-makers (Commies were not mentioned), the speakers believed that strip mining was a fine example of American progress. Referring to SOCM, one stripper rose in wrath: "In 1945, I was in the South Pacific fighting the Japs. I thought I was saving our Cumberland then. Maybe these people ought to go to Vietnam and really get down to saving our Cumberland." The jobs argument is a standard alibi by the stripping industry, but it is easily countered. At Lake City, a field representative for District 19 of the United Mine Workers Union, said that jobs and the economy would hardly suffer if stripping were banned. "There are such a few men working in the strip mines that if these mines were closed, the men could be absorbed in deep-mine work. If you go back a few years, you'll see that the strippers put out of work thousands of miners in Tennessee. It's strange. Now the strippers are suddenly concerned about jobs." *

* Ken Hechler spoke on the House floor September 22, 1971, on the jobs issue. "National Coal Association President Carl E. Bagge estimates that 24,000 men are employed in surface coal mines. Perhaps 4000 of these are employed in West Virginia, my state. Yet 19,000 West Virginians work in tourist and recreation industries, and they are entitled to their jobs too. As

What troubled Jimmy Sands most when he drove past the stripped mountain near Stinking Creek was that this particular one had been reclaimed. "That's what they tell us," he said sadly. "But look at it. It's destroyed forever. It will never be a mountain again, just a pile of rubble. If this is what they mean by reclamation, then we need a new word, not just a new mountain. Fixing it over with a few slithers of high grass isn't reclaiming it. Not in my eyes." Nor in the eyes of Ken Hechler. He has compared reclamation to "putting lipstick on a corpse."

The mountain people of east Tennessee who oppose strip mining are not articulate, nor do their knees bend to the gods of progress worshiped elsewhere. Thus, they can be passed off as hicks, or as romantics who still think mountains and streams are important. But dismissing a people is not the same as dismissing their values. The country's growing appetite for coal — often to run more and more machines that seem to be making us less and less happy — is being used as an example of a greater good that must allow a lesser evil. But how lesser is tearing up nature and how greater is the electric power that results? There is also the ethical problem of the free-enterprise system. Does it mean that strip miners should be free to use their enterprise to make money for themselves while making chaos for others? We have been mindlessly answering yes to that question, as if to challenge

strip mining increases, the attractiveness of West Virginia as a place to live and work, and also the tourist industry itself, will certainly decline.

"Those now concerned about jobs gave little attention to the 300,000 miners displaced when the underground coal mines were mechanized in the 1950s. Many of the jobs in strip mining are highly skilled occupations, easily transferable to road construction or housing. But strip mining is like taking seven or eight stiff drinks: you are riding high as long as the coal lasts, but the hangover comes when the coal is gone, the land is gone and the jobs are gone and the bitter truth of the morning after leaves barren landscape and a mouth full of ashes. The tourist and recreation potential of a stripped area is nil; in fact, far more jobs are provided for the future through protection of the environment."

parts of free enterprise was treason itself. But in preserving the institution of the free-enterprise system, little energy has been given to preserving anything else — least of all such defenseless treasures as rivers, mountains, wildlife. A few disturbers of the peace like Jimmy Sands and others in the Cumberlands are beginning to understand that free enterprise can also mean ruthless enterprise.

PART VI

Friendly Neighborhood Disturbers

Julius Andracsek

NOT ALL the nonadjusted people are disturbing the peace of mighty corporations or clever lobbies, nor are all of them found only beyond the rim of one's neighborhood. Sometimes they are men and women seen every day, perhaps doing little more than running a small business or only trying to make sense out of life by valuing one of its commoner parts. The values they care for, either by sweating for or sweating out, may not mean life or death but often they mean the difference between quality and cheapness.

Ever since my two oldest boys, Jimmy, four, and John, three, could walk, I had been taking them to the University Bake Shop on Wisconsin Avenue, near my home in northwest Washington. The bakery is in an amiable neighborhood, in the shadow of the Washington Cathedral, with a number of apartment buildings to the south and west, and heavy-set Cleveland Park houses to the north. The bakery was one of our regular stopoffs in a day of aimless poking around. My kids liked best the chocolate-chip cookies, and it was usually six of these that we bought every Saturday. Once, on a July afternoon of 97°, I tried some of the bakery's ice cream — a quart of vanilla for $1.70, packed into a white, unmarked, tube container. That night, my four-year-old was into only a few bites of it when he said to his younger brother, "Hey, this ice cream is different — you can chew it." The observation, like most others at a table shared by tired-out parents and babbling kids, was not recognized for any special genius, and it was quickly pushed offstage by chatter about the flowers on the table, the broken bicycle in the cellar, and when an uncle was coming to visit.

The next day, I was picking up a suit in a tailor shop and happened to stop next door at the bakery. I ordered an ice-cream cone. Usually, a crew of college girls works the counter, but today it was their lunch hour so the baker himself was taking customers. Julius Andracsek is in his early sixties, short, full-chested, with stubby fingers good for kneading bread, and usually wearing baggy white pants and a T-shirt. He has a stern face, full of dour ethnic authority but which regularly springs trap doors of humor in his conversation. No other customers were in the store, so we talked about his ice cream.

At first, he made no special claim about it, saying only that he made ninety gallons every Thursday. "That way," he said, "it is fresh for the weekend eaters who need something to pick them up." I remembered my boy's comment from the night before, and passed it along to Mr. Andracsek. "Your son — four years old — said my ice cream is different?" He laughed. "Well, let me tell you, you have a smart boy. Sure my ice cream is different. I use only five ingredients: fresh cream and milk from a dairy in Virginia, sugar, some salt, and pure flavoring. I make peach ice cream, just to show you, only when peaches are falling off the trees. I could use the canned puree that the salesmen keep coming around to hawk, but then you are fooling the customers. They think they're getting the real thing from nature, but they're only getting the phony thing from the factory. The season for peach ice cream is when nature has put the peaches on the trees. This happens in the summer, from early June to late August. I get my peaches fresh from the grower, chop them up, and put them into my ice cream. The people who buy it get fresh ice cream and they get fresh peaches. How can you do it any other way?"

Good question. For the next few months, I looked into the American ice-cream industry and discovered that there are plenty of other ways of doing it. According to the International Association of Ice Cream Manufacturers, in 1964 (the last year that figures are available), 732 million gallons of ice cream were produced. The association doesn't say how much of this was gunk or how much was quality ice cream as made by small operators like Julius Andracsek. The official word is not that important anyway. The consumer who cares about his ice cream knows how to make his own judgment. Superior ice cream is bitey, chewy, and heavy, is made with only a few basics, and costs plenty. Inferior ice cream, with as much chew as shaving cream, goes *puff* within the chamber of the mouth, a minor explosion of air as teeth cut into it because that is a main ingredient of inferior ice cream: air. Glop ice cream can be made with artificial flavoring and coloring, and may contain a long list of ingredients that the average ice-cream eater, in his innocent joy, has no idea exist, much less knows he is sliding into his stomach. These include gum acacia, plastic cream (the actual name), sodium carboxymethylcellulose, tetrasodium pyrophosphate, polyoxyethylene sorbitan tristearate, propylene glycol. As if these chemicals were not enough to sicken you, an ice-cream maker intent on turning out cut-rate slush can use old reliables like dried milk, corn syrup, whey, and water.

Only the rare consumer knows this. The Food and Drug Administration, with more on the market to worry about than a dairy product that can be merely synthetic, airy, and puffy, requires the manufacturer only to label any artificial flavoring. Even this modest requirement, according to a *Consumer Bulletin,* was once fought by the ice-cream lobby. Federal regulations set three main minimum standards: ice cream must be at least 10 per cent butterfat, not more than

50 per cent air, and a half-gallon must weigh at least two and a quarter pounds. The FDA Standard of Identity for ice creams gives the manufacturer twenty-six kinds of dairy products to choose from (if he doesn't like sweetened, condensed skim milk, for example, he can throw into the vat sweetened, condensed part-skim milk), thirteen sweetening agents (dextrose, lactose, fructose, and other names fit for the poetry of Ogden Nash), six forms of egg, five kinds of caseinates (milk-product chemicals) and some fifteen other items that help "stabilize." After the government spells all this out, the consumer is back where he started: both he and the manufacturer are on their own.

Some 1000 brands of ice cream are sold nationally, with most large cities like Washington or Chicago having from fifty to seventy-five brands available. The mildly alert consumer can cite the better-known brands: Howard Johnson's, Breyers, Baskin-Robbins, Good Humor, Louis Sherry, Meadow Gold, Sealtest, Lucerne (sold in Safeway stores), Heidi (sold in Giant stores). Out of all these frozen assets, though, only a few ice creams can satisfy the tastes of ice-cream heads, because only a few are made by artists using the real thing and who refuse to adjust to the methods of the mass-producing glop makers. Andracsek ice cream doesn't have to be eaten for its quality to be known. I took a pint of it one afternoon to a Safeway supermarket a few blocks away to weigh it on one of the unused check-out scales. It came to 17 ounces, container included. I went to the freezer and carried to the scale some other brands. A pint of Lucerne weighed 9 ounces. A Schrafft's pint was 12 ounces. Briggs "extra rich" ice cream weighed 11 ounces. The difference between Andracsek ice cream and these other brands is even more obvious when compared by weight in half-gallons. An Andracsek half-gallon weighs 68 ounces, almost double the federal minimum of 36 ounces. Lucerne weighs 41 ounces. Schrafft's, a company that likes to picture itself as quality conscious, comes into the flyweight ring at a rough-and-tough 49 ounces. The difference between Andracsek ice cream and mass-produced brands is air. Those who remember licking the dashers of a hand-cranked home freezer know that air is introduced into ice cream according to how much the ice cream is beaten. Andracsek mixes and beats for only twelve minutes, thus getting in only enough air to keep the ice cream from becoming dense and buttery. Some factory brands are so aerated that no bite or chew is left; the ice cream is like stroking an Angora cat — smooth and pretty but nothing there.

"I've never wanted to make ice cream any other way, although I know I could easily fool a lot of my customers," said Andracsek. "It's no big thing taking the kind of stand I do, I mean refusing to get in line with the junk-food makers. It's just a way of being faithful to a few things — myself, my sons, and maybe my past. When I first started out in the pastry business, I made the freshest and most pure ice cream I could because I had to. Every other baker in town was making it fresh and pure, and people wouldn't settle for anything less. You had to produce quality. Now it's changed. The big ice-cream makers have conditioned people to settling for airy, puffy stuff that squirts out of a tube from a giant vat. The older people who remember what good ice cream once was have gradually given up eating it, because they'd rather have no ice cream than bad ice cream. Meanwhile, the kids and younger people have come along. They eat the mass-produced stuff because they don't know any better. They've never eaten quality ice cream, so they think they're getting something good. And the big boys keep fooling them. Well, I think that's wrong. I can't do much about it, except not to become a part of it. It's no big struggle for me, and I'm no crusader by any means. But I'll keep on making pure ice cream because I think it needs to be done."

It definitely does. The ice-cream freezer in a Giant supermarket near the University Bake Shop carries three brands in half-gallons: Briggs, Heidi, and State House. The impression is given that these three companies make the three brands but by checking the nearly microscopic print on the container, the consumer can see that the District of Columbia, Maryland, and Virginia food-license numbers of Heidi and State House are identical with the numbers on a Briggs container. Thus, all three brands are made by the same manufacturer — Briggs. A call to the Giant headquarters gets the reluctant concession that this is true. A further comparison, and one with deeper implications, reveals that the weights of the three half-gallons are virtually identical: 42 ounces for Briggs and Heidi, 40 ounces for State House. But the prices are not identical. Briggs costs $1.19, Heidi $.99, and State House $.69.

Because ice-cream makers prefer not to list the ingredients or butterfat content, and the FDA lets them get away with this omission, the consumer, selecting among the three brands, has no way of knowing differences in quality or weight, only price. It is all ice cream, from the same maker at almost the same weight. Yet a difference of twenty cents exists between brand A and brand B, and a fifty-cent gulf between A and C. How is the consumer to know what he is getting for his money? Or which ice cream is superior? Giant supermarkets, which began in 1971 a well-publicized campaign to serve and inform the customer, is doing this in a curious way concerning ice cream. Or perhaps the company believes it is coming clean with the truth when it sticks a unit-pricing label on the ice-cream shelf. A label will say $.55 a pint and then in the weight-proportion blank, $1.10 a quart. Thanks loads.

The larger ice-cream companies deserve no special damnation for what they make. The glop is legal and the public will buy it. Moreover, it is cheap. A half-gallon of many brands can be bought for less than the $.85 that a pint of Andracsek ice cream costs. Though ice-cream consumption in the city of Washington equals the national annual intake of 15 quarts per person, only one manufacturer has a plant within the district — Briggs Ice Cream Company at 3621 Benning Rd., NE. A few days after talking to Julius Andracsek, I visited the Briggs operation. The plant covers six acres, employs some 100 persons five days a week on two shifts and, according to the management, produces four million gallons of ice cream yearly. This includes some sixty varieties, from ice-cream cones, cups, and popsicles to bulk. Briggs is a family-owned firm, controlled by three brothers long known in Washington for their successful meat business. They went into ice cream in 1954.

Most Washington-area supermarkets, as well as the delicatessens and small shops, carry the Briggs brand. I asked a Briggs official what they put into Briggs ice cream, but my question was clearly out of place. "Just say we use the finest ingredients," he said. He also declined to discuss the butterfat content. "Just say we make a fine product." In place of these topics that some ice-cream consumers consider important, the Briggs man talked about "the high-class country clubs and restaurants we supply. We're also the first producers in the area to come up with dietetic ice cream. We also make sherbets that are a hundred per cent butterfat free." In supermarket freezers, the Briggs containers are common. One of them is a quart package with *gourmet* on the label and marked clearly with the words *hand packed*. Ice-cream loyalists have known from the ice age that the hand-packed product is traditionally better in quality than the brick or prepacked variety — less air is allowed in because of the packing — and they are willing to pay more for it. While touring the plant with a PR man, I asked if he could show me the workers hand packing the

Briggs containers saying *hand packed.* "Well," said the
official, "just by coincidence they don't happen to be in at this
particular moment." Nor was he sure of their schedule, so
I couldn't see them any other time either. I asked if he would
describe how the hand packers go about hand packing.
"Sure," he said, strangely dropping his guard. A worker on
the assembly line "just holds it [the container] under the
filling machine. So there's a hand on the package as it is
packed. We say 'hand packed,' not 'hand dipped.' That's
pretty damned clever, isn't it?" Yes, indeed.

In the general marketplace of ice cream, the relationship
between low or high quality to low or high prices reflects the
new direction the product is taking — less of a food and more
of a snack. Once part of the traditional meal, the dessert, to be
eaten at table, millions now go to ice-cream parlors with the
blind ardor with which people visit hamburger or pizza joints.
Most cities now have specialized ice-cream parlors, selling
nothing else and packing in the crowds, like ice cream into a
small cup. Though well short of the excellence of pastry-shop
handmade ice cream, parlor ice cream usually has more taste
and grip than the average supermarket brand, and is priced
higher too. People flock to the parlors for another reason —
the lure of variety. Adults used to seeing boring restaurant
menus where ice cream appears at the bottom in only the
three old standards — vanilla, chocolate, or strawberry —
can sit in a parlor and unleash their whims on a
menu of *only* ice-cream choices. You feel liberated, even a
little wanton. The choice of nuts, syrups, sauces, toppings,
flavorings, and sprinklings usurps any cares of quality about
butterfat or air content. Moreover, self-indulgence is not
embarrassing, as it might be in a restaurant at dessert time,
because everyone else is stuffing it in also. Although the
service is what can be expected when the hungry hordes compete for the attention of young soda jerks and jerkettes at

these parlors, an hour and a few dollars spent eating ice cream sends gusts of pleasure blowing through the spirit in a way that a visit to a Howard Johnson's or Schrafft's never could.

Ice-cream freaks who really need emotional lifts go to Baskin-Robbins. As with Heinz' fifty-seven varieties of soup or Union's seventy-six oil products, Baskin-Robbins is visually identified with its thirty-one flavors. This number, however, is actually only a code word, which steady customers know really means unlimited flavors, with thirty-one of them guaranteed to be on sale at any given time. The *Guiness Book of World Records* lists Baskin-Robbins as marketing 401 flavors. Elements of mystery and intrigue are thrown at the customer in a choice of such flavors as tin roof, Waldorf salad, rocky road, alallie-berry, frootenany, here-comes-the-fudge, mai tai ice, and, for all those tired moms and dads on their second honeymoon or newly-weds on their first, passion fruit sherbet. Anyone with a little time can stake out a Baskin-Robbins parlor and observe the paradox that often the meekest-mannered people order the most bizarre flavors — and in double or triple scoops — while the most glazed freaks will ask for a single dip of vanilla. Either way, Baskin-Robbins cones are selling. In 1961, 40 million were consumed, while in 1970, the number jumped to 380 million.

Although Baskin-Robbins spokesmen, like the secretive men at Briggs, refuse to say what ingredients go into the ice cream they sell nationally in 780 stores — "we have a secret formula," said the local man — the basic facts include a reported 14 per cent butterfat and 12 ounces to the pint. This is well below the standards of Julius Andracsek. A recent study by advertising analysts from Ohio State and the University of Illinois examined Baskin-Robbins's success from the promotional angle. "The Baskin-Robbins product itself is an example of demand stimulation. Every effort is made to tempt the public appetite with exotic new flavors — flavors that no one had ever dreamed of. Vanilla, for example, becomes Pennant Winning Vanilla when combined with Umpire Style Razzberries and Nutty Cashews in Baseball Nut ice cream."

Elsewhere around the country, small unfranchised operators are doing well, though less spectacularly than the Baskin-Robbins chain. Much of what they sell depends on the customer's need to sit and idle his tense engine, as well as indulge his weakness for sauces and syrups; most of the parlor ice cream is of better quality than the glop dished out at roadside stands or the supermarket-freezer brands. Any doubters should compare visually the one flavor of ice cream that is most telling about a manufacturer's attitude to the public: vanilla fudge. Parlor vanilla fudge deftly ribbons the fudge around the interior mass of vanilla. The flavors balance, and with one bite you get the taste of two. The inexpensive brands fudge on using fudge, creating a thin and stringy mix. Instead of a balance you get a blend. If that's what you want, wait for the creatives at Baskin-Robbins to concoct Mulatto Spree.

In the open ice-cream competition, only the pastry-shop product — of which Andracsek ice cream is a model — can satisfy the pleasure needs of the ice-cream head. He knows it by taste, by weight, and by sticking his finger into it and having it come out crusted with ice cream, not clean, as it does with Howard Johnson's or even Baskin-Robbins's. It is useless getting overly alarmed at how much American ice cream is unworthy. Junk ice cream fits in well with all the waste and trickery of the other puffy, airy, and tasteless foods Americans stuff into themselves. That we demand so little from our ice cream is not so much a lapse in taste, as it is traceable to the few demands we make on other foods, even to the point of not demanding they be safe.

Eric Gill, an English craftsman and a member of the old Gilbert Chesterton–Hillaire Belloc–Ronald Knox circle, said once that eating inferior ice cream was a sin. He meant his remark not as a joke, the kind that bright Englishmen delight in, but offered it as a commentary on how we take our pleasure. No one gobbles a mouthful of ice cream for any of the more somber reasons he shovels in other foods, neither for nutrition, fashion, or survival. It is pleasure. To eat ice cream that is second, third, or last rate is to willfully take unpleasurable pleasure, an act that mars the self-honesty of the eater and degrades whatever style he has left. Ice cream is a pleasure that shoud be a full one, and anything less is a heavy fall from grace. In *The Decline of Pleasure,* Walter Kerr asks what happens to a man "when, for reasons of economy or perhaps just plain carelessness, he buys and spoons into himself ice cream short on real cream and shy of real flavor? In point of fact, we know what happens to him — because he is ourself and we do just that all the time. He comes to hate himself. He sits there eating, unable to resist the next mouthful because he has a memory of ice cream that once satisfied him deeply and because he is entitled to some kind of pleasure, and at the same time seething because it is perfectly clear to him that he isn't enjoying a single spoonful . . . He knows what he should do, of course; he should put the dish aside, leave half of it behind him. When he doesn't, which is most of the time, it is because he will not surrender the right to eat ice cream when the ice cream isn't worth eating."

Julius Andracsek has been saying the same all these years, except he's been holding out for excellence. "Americans aren't used to quality ice cream," he says. "Many of my customers are Europeans, people from the embassies in Washington, or just people in the neighborhood from the old countries. A European says: 'Make me some good ice cream, the best you can.' But the American says only, 'Make me some ice cream.' He's so adjusted to synthetics in his serious foods that he doesn't dream it can be any different with the so-called fun foods. That's the pity of it — the big manufacturers push synthetic and cheap ice cream. Americans eat it and think that's all there is to it. The package is gold-colored, printed in old English lettering, and a meadow painted on, so it must be all right. It must be the best."

Julius Andracsek does not give up on Americans, however much junk ice cream they waste their money on and eat. He believes quality can be learned. The only worry with this, though, is that there are so few around like him to teach us.

Fran Lee

ANOTHER OF THE PLACES I visit on Saturday with my children, after seeing the Andracseks in their bakery, is Turtle Park, a playground area a few blocks from my home in northwest Washington. It is called Turtle Park because its large children's sandbox has three giant cement turtles which the kids jump on, over, under, and around. The park is a still center in the neighborhood, a closed-in place with ample room, facilities, and beauty. Adults use it almost as much as the children — for family picnics, softball games, jogging, and loafing. Or at least the neighborhood people did use it. In the past few years, I have noticed a dropping-off, fewer people coming to use the park even though more families have moved into the area. No government survey has been made to determine the cause of this decline, but my own suspicion is that the park has gone to the dogs — literally. On some days, especially in the spring and summer, the park is little more than a dog run. Owners come with their animals, ranging from huge, restless Afghans to nervous toy poodles that pee every few yards, and set them loose in both the open field among the families or in the play area among the children. Many of the dogs, especially the larger breeds, need the exercise of a free run; living in an urban neighborhood, instead of a farm, they spend most of the day penned in a yard or locked indoors.

As justified a cause as dog liberation might be, Turtle Park has signs at both entrances saying NO DOGS ALLOWED. Some owners see the signs and do not come in, but others, who are irresponsible in their trust, ignore it. Aside from limbering their legs, the dogs inevitably limber their bowels and bladders, defecating on the sidewalks, grass, or in the children's sandbox. Some dogs, unleashed, trot over to defenseless infants in strollers and, before the mother or father can rush to the rescue, lick the startled child in the face. "He's just friendly," the dog owner usually says, when the parent pulls back the terrified child. Occasionally, a community-minded dog owner will come to the playground with his animal leashed. Once, I saw the rarest sight of all — an owner who scooped up the pile of excrement his dog deposited on the sidewalk. But these were exceptions; in the minds of many dog owners in the neighborhood, Turtle Park is as much for dogs as for citizens.

Over the years, a number of my dog-owning friends — a few are now former friends — have growled at me, "You don't like dogs, you're prejudiced." I hear the words in astonishment. The opposite is true. I respect and treasure dogs, from the American Kennel Club's best-of-show to the wandering strays with their difficulty in surviving. City dog owners who keep their pets leashed and quiet, who clean up behind them, and get rid of them when they bite someone — these people are a credit to both the dog world and the real world. Who could not enjoy the dog stories these James Thurbers and Jack Londons insist on telling you? Nothing lifts the mind more than listening to otherwise rational people who have this one craziness — their dog. They talk to it, eat with it, consult it for advice, get divorced over it, spend money on it, give it the run of their home, enjoy the power of owning a big dog or the fashion of a small dog, send it to boutiques for hair clips, lobby for better dog laws, even run their car off the highway rather than hit one. I'm for this, and stand on my hind legs for both these owners and their dogs.

It is the irresponsible owners who are troubling — the

owners who feel that their animal's convenience comes ahead of the community's claim to safety and health. As with most of us who let the small insanities slide toward us — the big insanities roll at us like tidal waves, and our energy must be used to brace for them or be swept off — I took no notice of the irresponsible dog owners until I was involved personally. It happened one weekend morning, early between eight and nine, while I was walking on the grassy outer rim of Turtle Park with the boys. About fifty feet ahead, near a clearing in a tree glade, a full-grown male German shepherd appeared. In violation of District law, the owner had no leash on the animal; he trailed behind, another full-grown male. On seeing the dog approaching, I picked up the children high in my arms. The dog neither barked nor showed its fangs, but the size of the animal alone, his romping around the tots and sniffing them, caused fright. Dog lorists say, never let a German shepherd know you fear it.

"Oh don't worry," called out the owner. "He won't bite. He just adores children." Perhaps, I said to myself. Nevertheless this was a playground for children with signs banning dogs and also a public place protected by the District of Columbia law requiring dogs to be on at least a four-foot leash.

"Could you call your dog off?" I asked.

"He's a friendly fella," the owner replied.

"I don't care how friendly you think your dog is," I said, "please get him away from my kids. This is a playground for children, not a run for unleashed dogs."

Startled by this statement, and perhaps angered because I was not taken by the charms of his dog, the master replied, "If that's your attitude, then no, I won't call off my dog. You're on your own, you bastard."

My kids by now were crying, sensing both the real enemy of the owner and the potential enemy of the dog. I carried them back to the street, 200 yards away, where my car was parked. The trip was harrowing. If I put the kids down, the dog would have come closer to investigate this well-guarded catch. On the other hand, if I ran too fast, I risked exciting the animal even more. The dog already seemed to sense that it had three frightened victims under its spell.

For sure, the owner did. He was like a king shouting to his army to put the enemy to flight. He called out, "Had enough yet, bastard? What's the matter, you afraid of a dog? Go ahead, you coward, run." I kept imploring and demanding that he call off his dog, but he did nothing and seemed to be enjoying the scene. I made it safely to the car — not without stepping in some freshly deposited dung, though — and went immediately to the local police precinct to report the incident. In telling my story to one of the police officers, I noticed an obvious lack of sympathy for the ordeal I had just escaped. It is true you don't go to the police for warm feelings but you do expect at least a mild grunt of concern. Instead, the cop's first words after I ran through it were, "You don't like dogs? What were you trying to do, frighten your kids? German shepherds are friendly dogs. You should know that." The implication of the cop's remarks could not have been clearer; I was the strange one, not the dog owner. I pressed on by saying that some shepherds are doubtlessly friendly and some are not, but the point was that two laws had been broken and was anyone going to look for the law-breaking owner. He answered by asking for my identification. I gave him a driver's license and Washington *Post* press card. "With the *Post*." He snorted. "I should have known. You guys get everything wrong." With a warning not to bother any neighborhood dogs again, he told me to get going. I learned later that this particular cop had once been a trainer for the force K-9 squad.

Challenging the irresponsibility of dog owners is a work that few take seriously, and even then it can only be part-time work. Playground peace or sidewalk cleanliness are hardly major city problems, not when rats infest tenements, or when the highway lobby continues to lay down more roads, or when the stores sell flammable clothing for kids. It is better to battle where the abuses are more dangerous; what is a mound of dung in Turtle Park, or an unleashed dog, compared to the automobile industry making defective cars that might kill you and which have killed others? Yet the dung and the dogs are still there, plus their owners whose irresponsibility causes the abuse. To ignore them, to throw a tantrum rather than throw a block, is to let life be cheapened in still another daily devaluation.

When I wrote a story in the *Post* about my experience in Turtle Park, one of those I heard from was Fran Lee. She is a New York woman who founded and runs the valuable organization Children Before Dogs (15 West 81st Street, New York, New York). Before this, Miss Lee — along with writers like Sidney Margolius — was one of the first real-article consumer advocates in the country. She was talking about frauds and deceptions long before Ralph Nader or Bess Myerson had even dreamed that some of the generals and captains of industry might be duping us. For many years, Miss Lee was the only consumer editor on American radio on a steady basis. She didn't last though. She says attempts were made to censor some of her shows, so she resigned. She told a reporter at the time — in late 1969 — that "commercial stations should get credit when they do good things. WNEW allowed me to tell it like it is. But the manufacturers began screaming bloody murder and then the nervous executives, salesmen, and the ad men got into the act. I started getting pressured and badgered. Lawyers began trying to take things out of my scripts. I was working fourteen hours a day. Everybody thought I was making millions, and all I was making was heartaches — for myself. One day, my boss said to me, 'Fran, I love your integrity but I can't afford it.' That did it. I'd rather have unemployment than have lawyers censor my scripts."

Miss Lee began disturbing the peace of New York after walking along Fifth Avenue one morning in January 1968, stepping in dog dung, and falling to the pavement. "I'll never forget it," she said. "I was wearing a mink coat and the excrement sunk deep into the fur. With most of the torments in New York, you can somehow strike back — curse out the taxi driver who nearly runs you over, heckle the politicians when they come around to grovel for votes, argue with the merchants who try to dupe you. But with dog dung, what can you do? It's an anonymous insult. You can never find the owner who let his dog pollute the street. How can you shout back at him, or maybe shove him in dung himself?"

Cooling it is the original New York art form, but this time Miss Lee opened wide the vents of her heated anger. She researched and discovered that New York City had 500,000 dogs whose contribution to the community was 50,000 tons of dung a year and some 5 million gallons of urine. Many others in New York shared Miss Lee's disgust at the filth but no one had organized a citizens' group. "I formed Children Before Dogs," she says, "because that was the problem reduced to its essence. Do we want the city to be a place to raise our kids or to be a kennel? I remember a meeting we had early on in my apartment. I had invited some dog owners. Things were quiet for a while but then the discussion became a true Manhattan dog fight. In high rage, one of the owners shouted at me — what are you trying to do in New York, put children before dogs? He had become so irrational about his pet that he actually believed the community should give it priority over human beings."

For the past few years, Miss Lee has been going about the country, unleashed, trying to alert people to the health hazards and social inconvenience of dogs, and telling people that human rights come before dog rights.

When Miss Lee showed at the Washington *Post* one morning early in 1972, she asked for my office, but the guard at the main-entrance desk wouldn't let her past. At sixty-two, dressed like a supercrow in shiny colors and sparkling jewelry — which she doesn't buy from the merchants but fashions herself from loose ends — and all of it under a hat with brims like pelican wings, she is high on the Pinkerton list of "keep outs." The guard called me on the intercom and said, "A lady, I mean, someone named Fran Lee, is here. She says she has a meeting with you. That so?" It's all right, Straight Arrow, let her pass.

Newspaper offices are regularly being visited by citizens who believe reporters are trays on which to serve the public solutions to all the problems the news columns describe. Often no way exists to distinguish between the person who has a problem and deserves a hearing and the person who has a neurosis and deserves a psychiatrist. Reporters have an obligation to be available to as many readers as possible, but one screening method I have is whether the caller comes in the morning or the afternoon. If the afternoon, it suggests they have little understanding of the news business, because this is when the guillotine of the deadline begins falling and no reporter cares to talk to anyone but his sources. If they appear in the morning, then you figure the caller at least is considerate enough of the reporter's schedule to come when the hour is relaxed, even if the caller isn't. Miss Lee came in the morning, so we talked.

She is a whole house of fervor, with east and west wings stored with frankness. "Sure, you learned something at Turtle Park," she said when I told her about my experience. "Just because there's a sign up saying NO DOGS doesn't mean a thing. The animals are chained up or locked in most of the time, so taking them to the park in the evenings or weekends is natural. Just because kids and people are there doesn't stop them. The dog is the master. If you speak up and say otherwise, you're un-American. You'd be better off attacking apple pie."

Ardor is not easy to accept in Washington. The person who pries open the tightest vents of emotion is often suspected of being out of control. He hasn't learned reasoning yet, so leave him be. Pretend you're deep in private thought when you meet him or perhaps say you'll mention the problem to a friend whose department handles it. It was easy to appreciate Fran Lee from the beginning because she had an overflow of ardor that she offered to share, not impose. She cared little about winning anyone over, but in delighted elation wanted only to pass along the information she knew.

"Dogs that frighten your kids in Turtle Park are bad enough," she said, "but what about diseases you can get from dogs? *Toxocara canis* is a parasitic disease we are only learning about now. It's the roundworm. When you hear about a puppy being wormed, that's what they're trying to get out. If the larvae of the worm are swallowed — say by a child at a playground sandbox who touches dog dung with his fingers and later puts the fingers in his mouth — it can find its way to the liver, spleen, even work its way to the brain and into the eyes. Some worms have been found in the heart. You don't hear about toxocara too much because the doctors and the vets haven't done their homework. For example, a friend of mine had an eighteen-month-old baby who was very sick with convulsions. At the hospital, the doctors thought he had meningitis and treated him for all sorts of things. Finally, just before a tumor operation was scheduled, the doctor noticed the family kept a puppy on the back porch and he suspected toxocara canis. And it was. The baby was riddled with worms. A year and a half later, the child is hyperactive and still convulsive, but the doctors hope he'll be all right. Sometimes, the effects of toxocara are not serious. The worm dies before it does a lot of damage. But eyes often get ruined and have to be removed. And the tragedy is that many doctors do not recognize toxocara. They think it glaucoma or detached retina."

A major fear of a journalist is being duped, of being a patsy for dubious facts. He is paid not only to report what he can find out but also to be suspicious about the high polish that sources often shine their statements with. In the weeks following Fran Lee's visit, I was able to research the dog problem and see that her statements were colored only by the safe tones of truth. In Atlanta, at the National Communicable Disease Center, Dr. Irving Kagan was alarmed at the health danger caused by dogs. He said that 20 to 40 per cent of all dogs in America are infected with the ascarid worm. He described it as a parasite similar in size to the earthworm and which grows in the dog's intestines. It is passed out with the feces. "If the dog chooses or is allowed to defecate in a playground, a play area, or a back yard," Dr. Kagan said, "there is nothing to keep children from coming into contact with the eggs in the waste. The kids, especially those in poverty areas, get it on their hands and pass it into their bodies when putting their hands into or near the mouth. When the child ingests the egg, the larvae settle into the usual body organs, especially the liver." Illnesses caused by contact with dog feces are not rampant, Dr. Kagan said, but they are common.

Kagan is a public official paid to watch for disease but the obscure medical journals also know about toxocara. A volume called *Diseases of Man Acquired from His Pets* by Balideo Bisseru states that "the public health problem presented by toxocara infections . . . in man is an important one, with further research and information called for." Some of this research was performed by a team of biologists who conducted a survey in Schenectady County, New York. Over a three-year period, a thorough examination of 64 dogs taken after gassing from the County Animal Shelter was made. Both male and female dogs from two weeks old to one year were included, half of them family pets and half strays. Amazingly, the examination revealed that 73.4 per cent of the dogs had toxocara canis. "The high prevalence of infection in 73.4 per cent of dogs in the survey should be emphasized," said the biologists,* "since some observers are of the opinion that an incidence of 7 per cent must be considered to be hazardous to the human population. Personal communications with three practicing veterinarians in the Schenectady area revealed that 80 to 90 per cent of all puppies are infected with roundworms." In the July 1971 issue of *To-day's Health,* a magazine of the American Medical Association, it was reported that "dog manure harbors the worm toxocara canis, which can cause lung disease, blindness and brain damage if ingested by children. Early this year, after playing with dog dung, a baby in Connecticut suffered permanent brain damage; a little girl in Pennsylvania lost the sight of an eye." In Houston, Dr. Clark P. Read, chairman of the biology department at Rice University, said that "we have turned up 30 cases of [diseased] liver here in the past five years, all of which are attributable to dog worms. From the standpoint of clinical disease, this means that there are probably 300 cases — at a minimum — in this area. These are, for the most part, children below the age of two."

As a disturber of the peace, Fran Lee is easily passed off as a nut and as a dog hater. Anyone who hates animals is

* Twitty J. Styles, Ph.D., and Dana S. Evans, M.S., in the New York state *Journal of Medicine,* December 1, 1971.

automatically insane. But she doesn't hate dogs, as I learned during a day spent with her in New York. Several times, in front of her apartment across from the Hayden Planetarium on 81st Street, neighbors with dogs stopped to chat with Miss Lee. The talking was friendly and no pro-dog or anti-dog remarks were exchanged. "These are the responsible owners," she said later in her attractive apartment. "How can you object to them? They keep the animals on leashes, out of the parks, and train them to defecate on paper in the apartment. If every dog owner in New York did that, I could worry about the things I used to — cyclamates, baby food, toothpaste, all the things consumers are being cheated on."

For years, Miss Lee had been one of the few New Yorkers who refused to adjust to the city's cesspool conditions. In the spring of 1972, evidence appeared that others were joining her. August Hechscher, head of Parks, Recreation and Cultural Affairs, announced that dogs must be kept out of playgrounds and zoos and some parks. These areas, he said, were intended for people, not dogs. A city law banning dogs from these areas already existed, but New York's policemen have seldom enforced it. Coinciding with the Hechscher move was the statement of Mayor John Lindsay, that the parks often "look like a pig pen" after the weekends. (Actually, pigs are among the cleanest of animals, not to mention pig owners, who know the value of a sanitary pen.) Lindsay added that the owners should have their dogs relieve themselves on a paper in the family bathroom, not in public places. Although banning dogs in playgrounds and zoos is a positive move, it does not really solve the problem. The irresponsible owner will now let his dog defecate elsewhere, grandly assuming he stays out of the parks in the first place. With this in mind, Jerome Kretchmer, head of the Environmental Protection Administration, asked for city legislation that would require the owner to scoop up his dog's excrement immediately after deposit. This is a bold reform for New York — where the dog lobby is strong — but scoop-the-poop laws are nothing new. Town councils in Nutley, New Jersey, Malverne, New York, and Shaker Heights, Ohio, had recently passed them, and politicians there report a new era of cleanliness. These towns are the exceptions, though, with most cities relying instead on seldom enforced curb-your-dog laws. "What does this do, though?" Miss Lee asks. "Instead of polluting the sidewalk, the dung pollutes the street. Somehow, this is seen as acceptable, overlooking two small facts: the dung is either washed by rain into the sewers untreated and from there into the rivers, or else it must be shoveled away by the garbage man or street cleaner. So in some neighborhoods you have the blacks and Puerto Ricans, and some ethnics like Italians, cleaning up after the middle- and upper-class white man. But the insult is even worse, because it is the white man's dog that is being cleaned."

In public meetings, Miss Lee is pushy, tart, and abrasive. For a while, she so aroused the hatred of the dog freaks that police protection was given when she went to give speeches. Rather than argue with her — how can you argue facts? — many New Yorkers try to laugh her off. William Buckley tried for some smiles in a column where he referred to the "fanatical gleam in [the] prose" of Miss Lee. Rather than getting exercised about the dog droppings, Buckley said, "Why couldn't they [American industries] develop a can of squirt which deodorizes it all, or better still, turns it into corn flakes, or the nearest alchemical achievement du Pont can come up with?" What is a joke for Buckley may be less funny to the many blind people in the city who step in the dung because they cannot see it, or the parents of babies who get toxocara, or the many elderly who don't go near the parks anymore because the dogs have taken over. Even James Wechsler, whose head is clear about so many issues, tried to reduce the dog problem as a pointless fight between dog lovers and dog haters. He wrote that "the dog issue is a perennial red herring . . . It is open season on dogs again, a recurrent hysteria that, one might say, intermittently sweeps certain sectors of the city when politicians and some of their constituents despair of solving large problems." Wechsler says he could conform to the scoop-the-poop law "but the spectacle of streets crowded with citizens carrying home such trophies [dung in plastic bags] is hardly my vision of a model city." Wechsler did not say what kind of a city New York will be if, with 500,000 dogs, the excrement stays on the streets, sidewalks, and grass.

New York's dog problem is not a major crisis, but a significant number of people are joining Fran Lee in believing that fighting back is better than adaptation. The resistance by some dog owners even to admit a problem exists, let alone cooperate to solve it, is perhaps traceable to the popular notion that environmental and health problems are always caused by some vague institution or corporation conveniently far off someplace. It is never oneself who may be cheapening or befouling the community, least of all one's relationship with a "harmless" pet. Miss Lee continues to travel the country, speaking to groups who still believe the citizens have power. But with dog food being part of a $1.4 billion industry in 1971, as compared to $390 million in baby food, the dog lobby is not about to roll over and play dead for anyone like Fran Lee. Her struggles against irresponsible dog owners continues. I hope that more journalists keep their mornings open when Miss Lee comes to town. If so, maybe Turtle Park will be returned to the people some day, along with all the other parks, playgrounds, zoos, and sidewalks Fran Lee cares about.

Jerry Kerr

BABYSITTERS USUALLY HAVE little to say when you drive them home. "How's your dad?" I asked the twelve-year-old who had watched our two boys, right after I asked her, "How's school?" The latter was fine. So was her father. "But he just quit his job. He's around the house a lot now. Mom likes it. So do we." I asked why he quit. "Oh, I don't know. He told us at dinner one night, but I forget. It was kind of solemn. He said he had to follow his conscience."

A few days later, while walking home, I ran into Jerry Kerr bringing groceries from his car into the house. The Kerr home is on Davenport Street in northwest Washington, not far from, and midway between, Wisconsin Avenue and American University; it is a middle-class family neighborhood with houses in the $35,000–$60,000. My own home was only a block from Jerry Kerr's but in the suburban isolation that keeps neighbors from knowing each other, we had never met. After an evening of talk with him — he invited me in after the groceries were settled — the story of a conscience came out. Kerr's story is important not because of its drama, but because it was deceptively undramatic: an antiwar conscience formed in the middle of suburban America, amid security, family, and the herd. In many ways, what Kerr did had as much, possibly more, of the heroic to it than similar choices of consciences made by the draft resisters and the Catholic left underground. Kerr is middle-aged, he lives with no safety-net of a religious order under him, and he has no companions from the neighborhood to provide the comfort of numbers.

A 1948 graduate of Middlebury College in Vermont, Kerr spent four years in the Navy, mostly in a Pacific fleet combat group that produced films and newsreels during the Korean war. He enjoyed the film-making and after the service came to Washington to continue working in films. In 1959, with experience in a private company, Kerr joined the Naval Photographic Center, writing and planning films in what soon became the heyday of Defense Department movie-making. He left in 1964 to film for the Interagency Committee for Oceanography. An offer from NASA came in 1966 and Kerr worked there for three years. In early 1969, he shifted to the Navy Department. His salary by then had reached a grade level of $21,000, a comfortable income to support his wife and four daughters.

One evening, about six months after starting work for the Navy Department, Kerr was driving into town on Massachusetts Avenue from Wisconsin Avenue, past the embassies and over Rock Creek Park. He had picked up an American University student, a hitchhiker on his way to a marshals' meeting for a Saturday peace demonstration, one of the larger ones that year that promised a gathering of 200,000. The two talked about the war, the march, and the military, Kerr chatting from casual amiability and the student speaking from passionate interest. Nearing the South Vietnamese embassy at 22nd and Massachusetts, Moore unexpectedly found himself caught in traffic, bottled up from Dupont circle. A frantic crowd of students suddenly came running along the avenue, with the police in pursuit. Soon everyone was caught in the clouds of tear gas. Kerr received the fumes full on. Choked and blinded, he was led away to a relief station by his hitchhiker, a veteran of gassings who knew the right footwork.

Kerr received relief for his eyes and lungs, but relief for his suddenly agonized consciousness did not come as easily. For the first time Kerr felt the war in a personal, nonabstract way. "I tasted a little of Vietnam's horror when I swallowed the gas," he recalled. "A part of me changed. I felt the violence, however mild and temporary it was. We have never had a foreign invasion on our soil, so we have abstracted war. It is a word without meaning — we talk about war the way we refer to the economy or the Church or the school system. All of these things are out there, never next to me. And definitely not in me."

After the gassing incident in November 1969, Kerr tried pushing it from his mind. By now, though, detailed news of the Mylai Massacre began appearing, and instead of one event's being pushed out, the second horror joined it to make Kerr's conscience doubly uneasy. "I thought only other nations and their armies murdered children point blank," he said, "but now I learned that Americans did it, too." If Kerr slept less calmly, his waking hours were comforted by enjoyment in his new work. He received an important writing and directing assignment on the film *The Brown Water Navy,* a dramatization of the Navy's role in the Mekong Delta of Vietnam. At first, Kerr wrote and directed it from Washington, and even received warm praise from E. R. Zumwalt, then on the way to becoming chief of naval operations. Zumwalt, known for his tolerance of long haircuts on seamen and other breaks with military tradition that Navy publicists call "daring," took a personal interest in the film; it would tell the public that the Navy also was a part of the Vietnam "success," not just the Army, Marine Corps, and Air Force. This was in January 1970.

In May, Kerr went on location in the Mekong Delta, a trip that was to become the third torch that eventually set him on fire against the war. "I remember the first day in the Me-

kong waterways," he recalled. "The area had exquisite
beauty. It had greens and vistas I'd never seen anywhere.
But then I took a helicopter ride. From above, the land was
hideous — bomb craters pock-marked the hills, the tree line
had become acres of stumps, the forests were scarred with
defoliant. If Americans had done this to the land — de-
stroying it to save it — what must we have done to the people?"

Kerr returned to Washington a stunned man. Feeling that
the war was wrong and that filming it in a favorable docu-
mentary only mocked his profession, he tried during the late
summer of 1970 to stop the film. On October 30, against the
pleas of his wife and the advice of his friends, Kerr wrote a
protesting memo to a superior, concluding simply, "I cannot
in conscience do any further work on this project." He did
not last long after that, little to his surprise. Shortly there-
after, he joined the growing number of unemployed Americans, although most of these would have said Kerr was crazy,
because he quit his job purposely.

"I had to leave," he said. "My position differed in no way
from the young men who resist the draft on grounds of conscience or refuse to carry out illegal orders. At stake, though,
and more basic to living with myself, was the authenticity of
the horror I felt at the gassing on Massachusetts Avenue, at
Mylai, at the scene from the helicopter in Vietnam. What
did my revulsion toward those events mean if I didn't become revolted at my own part in *The Brown Water Navy*?
They were all links in the same chain."

Kerr modestly disclaimed any uniqueness to his act. But
what it said to his friends was clear: a man cannot have a
part-time conscience, working feverishly on one moral issue
but then flagging on another. The informed conscience is
not an instrument of picking and choosing, coming down
hard on the safe questions of morality but ducking ones that

mean personal risk — in Kerr's case the risk of security. "How could I say no to Mylai but not say no to *The Brown Water Navy*? Both were part of the same atrocity, both were wrong. To pick Mylai and not the film would be to separate myself from the victims of that killing. In other words, let them suffer but not me." This kind of thinking made Kerr exactly the kind of prized convert for which the best parts of the peace movement — such as SANE or the Women's Strike for Peace — had been working for all those years, and still do work for: the comfort-bound, middle-class citizen who always balanced like a barbell the belief that his leaders knew best with the feeling that America was a humane country that cared only about peace.

After he left the war machine of the government, Kerr was a less tense man who now enjoyed his family and children in new ways. He was a lone protestor, and unsure of the next moves. But he began reading the newspapers more closely and had begun reading the books of Bernard Fall and others. As for the war, he said one afternoon while raking the leaves, "People think we're winding it down now. Look at the low casualty rate, they say, look at the foot soldier coming back, the Vietnamization. But what they don't understand is that America still has an enormous war machine in Southeast Asia, that the same mentality is running it, and the same urge to keep it going at full speed and full horror are still present. The air war is immense. The bombers are into Laos and Cambodia. 'Protective reaction,' says the military. And then Nixon tells us that we have to keep the bombs dropping until the last man leaves. Well, the destruction persists. We've let ourselves be conned into believing that the war is ending. Worse, we want to be conned. To be done with it, to get back to being the good humane Americans we've always thought we were. As for all those billions for ABM, Polaris, Poseidon, A-bombs, and H-bombs, well, what is that except juicing up for the next war?"

The particular protest of Jerry Kerr did nothing to stop the war. Almost daily, since the spring of 1972 and through the summer, bombing reports come from Vietnam and the Pentagon as though the raids were a track-and-field event, with new world records set by our athletes of the air: "the heaviest air strikes ever," "the most massive bombing assaults in the history of the war," "the most bridges blown out in a single day." It is clear by now that no single citizen, or even group of citizens, has the power to stop the bombing, no matter how heavy the flow of evidence that North Vietnamese civilians are being killed and their livelihood destroyed. At first, in the spring of 1972 when the bombing began, it looked as though Richard Nixon might only be another American President "getting tough," like Harry Truman ordering A-bombs dropped on Hiroshima and Nagasaki. But Richard Nixon was not hot under the collar; he was cool of mind, dug in, intending to carry out his promises of bombing until the North Vietnamese gave out.

In the face of all this, a fatalistic anguish could be felt among citizens like Jerry Kerr. What works? It almost appeared as if a new club competition had been created: who can devise the most original style of protest? During the summer of 1972, a group of cellmates at a Connecticut prison perched on the water tower calling for an end to the war. A group of writers lay down in the U.S. Capitol and refused to leave — an old trick but the writers were new faces. A Boston woman paid $15,000 for full-page ads in twelve Ohio newspapers in hopes of starting a flood of stop-the-bombing mail to the President. A senator's wife, Mrs. Philip Hart of Michigan, announced she was paying no more taxes, as a protest to the war.

Those who believe more bombs and more death to the North Vietnamese were the ways to peace were, in the surface sense, the lucky ones. They believed in a faith seldom doubted, so they remained untroubled while others like Kerr were filled with shame and squirmed with doubt about what their government was doing in their name. The haunting truth of an Ibsen remark could hardly be denied: "A person shares the responsibility and the guilt of the society to which he belongs." Thus, rather than clear the air of bombs, much of the antiwar protest appeared directed toward an equally noble goal: clearing the conscience of the antiwar citizen. For years the phrase *good German* has been a part of the idiom. Its meaning is clear: while the Nazi government went about killing six million Jews, few Germans questioned its policies and fewer still protested them. The destruction was accepted by the citizens as they went on with normal living. In this country there is a chance that in twenty, thirty, or fifty years, the phrase *good German* will be replaced by *good American.*

There is no strict analogy between the political leaders of America in the 1970s and those of Germany from 1938 to 1945, if only because the final numbers on our atrocities are not yet in. Even if they were, there is still the question of what do moral denunciations of Richard Nixon and his war council gain, except perhaps to make the denouncer feel morally superior — which may not be the case anyway. The issue is less who is dropping the bombs that are killing people and ruining a landscape than where the money comes from that allowed the slaughtering to go on. This implicates all but a few Americans who pay taxes; the money for destruction comes from the pockets of tax-paying citizens. Their money may not be sent to the government with a note saying, "Here's my bombing money, kill well with it," but it is being used for that nonetheless. Many accounts of wartime Germany insist that the citizens actually had no knowledge of the government's atrocities. The press was controlled and reports from the death camps were by rumor or unreliable word of mouth. Something might have been wrong, but, unlike accounts in American newspapers, no pictures showed the bombed buildings, the crippled and burned children, the mothers weeping over their dead.

Why did a few people like Jerry Kerr continue to protest the war when the protests clearly had no effect? Kerr believed that his act was, first, a rejection of despair. Second, it was an embracing of the importance of personal conscience when the collective conscience appeared to be falling apart. "North Vietnam is far away," he said, "and I can't control what is happening there. But at least I can control what is near — in my own conscience." At least something valuable was being guarded. No doubt, some of those who gained attention over the years with their antiwar zeal were mere actors in their own street theater. One year they were conscience-striken by America's pollution, the year before that by the conditions among migrant workers, maybe next year lead-paint poisoning among ghetto kids will choke them up. Then, also, the antiwar movement had been in trouble ever since the peace symbol began showing up in costume jewelry. People could take a stand — a fine safe one — by dressing up with peace earrings or a peace tie clasp. It is less sweaty to make your point that way than by quitting your job. Fittingly, when high officials spoke out against the war protesters, they inevitably hauled out what they saw as the cruelest insult: to cast doubt on the protesters' standing as Americans. Thus, question or condemn the acts of a bomb-happy President and you're a bad American. Exactly. Twenty years from now, or whenever the sun of the sad Vietnam day has finally set, the clearest conscience may belong to the citizen who can look back and say: *I refused to be a good American.*

Unlike many acts of conscience in the antiwar movement, Jerry Kerr's defiance was noiseless. No cameras recorded him handing in his resignation; he flashed no V sign; he made no denunciation of the President, the Pentagon, or the

CIA. He only explained to friends, his wife (who worked and could support the family), and his children the reason for his action. He continued to shop at the local Safeway, rake leaves in the fall, and go to the beach in the summer. And he could live with his conscience. It was not the best way to be a family man on Davenport Street, but for Kerr, it was the only way.